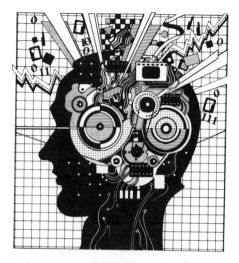

IDEA 1
EXCHANGE
Writing What You Mean

Linda Lonon Blanton
University of New Orleans

Newbury House Publishers
A division of Harper & Row, Publishers, Inc.
Cambridge, New York, Philadelphia, San Francisco, Washington, D.C.
London, Mexico City, São Paulo, Singapore, Sidney

Sponsoring Editor: Laurie Likoff
Production Coordinator: Cynthia Funkhouser
Text Design and Cover Design: Suzanne Bennett Associates
Text Art: Ray Skibinski
Compositor: Waldman Graphics
Printer and Binder: Malloy Lithographing Inc.

Newbury House Publishers, A Division of Harper & Row, Publishers, Inc.
Language Science
Language Teaching
Language Learning

Library of Congress Cataloging in Publication Data

Blanton, Linda Lonon, 1942–
    Idea exchange.

    1. English language—Rhetoric.   2. English
language—Textbooks for foreign speakers.   I. Title.
PE1408.B526   1988   808′.042   87-35014
ISBN 0-06-632614-1 (v. 1)

Printed in the U.S.A.
63-26144

First printing: March 1988

91 90 89 88 9 8 7 6 5 4 3 2 1

PREFACE

IDEA EXCHANGE: *Writing What You Mean* is intended for adult and young adult students of English as a Second Language. Its development has been greatly influenced by the evolution of composition theory over the last several years, and is the result of my own classroom experience in successfully applying current theory as I have worked to involve ESL students in the process of writing English in a nonthreatening, supportive way—one that is within their level of competence yet does not insult their intelligence. This book can be used successfully with high-beginning students, who may have to stretch—and that is good—as well as those at the intermediate level and above.

The lessons in the book are not self-instructional; they presume the guidance of a professional teacher. Following the table of contents is an introduction to the teacher that gives suggestions on how the materials may best be used. I urge anyone using this book to read that section.

The book is divided into ten units. Each unit contains prewriting and prereading activities; illustrated sample student essays with accompanying exercises; instructions for the student's own writing, within a process that promotes the development of all language skills; and a postwriting activity. For lower-level ESL writers, I have found that the writing process is of equal importance to the product, and the lessons are designed to show ESL students strategies for generating ideas and shaping them into a form that can be read and understood by someone else. The lessons are designed to guide students in their writing development to a point where they can generate several pages of written English.

I believe that it is important for students to begin the writing process early in their study of English, without waiting until they are more fluent. When it is done without fear of failure, writing can aid their overall progress in English. In other words, students will be writing English in order to learn more English.

I dedicate this book to my father, the late Seth Lonon, whose manner was so quiet and life so ordinary that I almost failed to recognize how very special he was.

I want to thank my student writers, Hassen Souissi, Lien Lo, Sebastian Pastor, and Cherry Cappel, whose essays form the core of each chapter of the book. Not only have they contributed authentic written language, but a whole lot of spirit as well.

I would like to acknowledge Ann Raimes for her term "parallel writing"; Flower and Hayes for pointing out some of the specific concerns that writers need to have for their readers; and Amy Sonka, for her concept of interaction in the classroom. I am undoubtedly indebted to many others whose ideas and terminology I've incorporated so thoroughly into my thinking that I am unaware of my debt.

Linda Lonon Blanton
New Orleans

TOPICS

TABLE
OF CONTENTS

TO
THE TEACHER

INTRODUCTION TO THE BOOK

Idea Exchange, Book 1, is written to the student. The student is addressed directly, and the instructions for each lesson are written as simply as possible so that they can be understood by the student, with just a little help from you. The purpose of addressing the students directly is not to leave you out, for you are indispensable, but rather to engage students by involving them personally in the materials, thereby making your job a little easier. You are invited to supplement, rearrange, and simplify where you see fit; only you know your students' needs and modes of learning and the constraints of your program.

What follows is a discussion of the methodology inherent in the materials, as well as a suggested plan for using them. These may help you in understanding why and how to use the lessons.

ASSUMPTIONS AND INTENT

The materials in *Idea Exchange, Book 1,* are based on the supposition that writing competency develops along a continuum of ever-increasing accuracy and fluency, and that it develops over time and within an atmosphere of encouragement and respect. Further, it develops most rapidly when the focus is on communicating and sharing ideas and experiences, not on counting errors and getting grades—although students certainly want feedback on their errors and rewards for work well done. Finally, writing competency develops when reading is intertwined with writing: readings then serve as a source of ideas, stimulation, vocabulary, and general usage that enables the reader to become a writer and, in turn, to be read.

Idea Exchange, Book 1, is designed for students of English as a

Second Language who have a high-beginning or low-intermediate level of proficiency. Because these materials may be your students' first formal instruction in writing English, the tone set by the materials you use, as well as the atmosphere created by you in using them, is extremely important.

My own experience in working with emerging ESL writers and in being a beginning writer in other languages tells me that inexperienced writers feel extremely vulnerable. My sense is that writing teachers, who need a great deal of patience and understanding in most circumstances, need an extra measure when working with students who are groping for a footing in the language.

You need to be adept at knowing when to intervene in the developmental process because students are on the wrong track and when to "wait it out" as students work through problems that only they can solve over time. A concern for the feelings of beginning writers and a strong sense of how ragged the course of writing development can be has influenced the wording, sequencing, and contents of the book.

Idea Exchange, Book 1, is written for adults who want to learn English for professional, academic, and business purposes. The format has been used successfully with high-beginning students, ranging in age from seventeen to forty-five, from eight different language backgrounds, and with varying degrees of education.

The book is divided into ten units or lessons. Each lesson contains prewriting and prereading activities, two illustrated readings with accompanying exercises on various aspects of the readings, instructions for the students' own writing, and a postwriting activity. In all, the ten lessons provide fifty to sixty class hours of instruction and writing practice.

THE LESSONS: PREWRITING

The first activity in each unit is journal writing. Its purpose is to give students the space and time in which to write, to connect thoughts and words without being concerned with how their writing appears. When students write in their journals, they are writing for and to themselves. Any notebook can become a "journal" when entries are made in it routinely. Another prewriting activity directs students to play with words; with this activity, students will find that they can be creative with their new language and have some fun with it. As they play with the language, they concentrate on meanings and word relationships.

The readings that follow in each unit are essays written by real students—three non-native speakers of English and one native speaker—and edited to suit this book. Despite the editing, the student writers' own voices and personalities are clearly expressed in their essays.

I have used student essays for three main reasons: to provide authenticity in the writing, to give students real people to identify with, and to engage them in using English to find out more about four individuals whom they will find interesting and worth caring about. The readings are considered part of the prewriting phase of each lesson as students interact with the ideas of the four student writers and begin to shape their own ideas.

The illustrations that accompany the readings can help clarify meanings. You may want students to follow along as you "tell" the readings. In turn, the illustrations can guide oral discussion or the retelling of each essay.

The readings are intended as readings, not models for your students' writing. Although the readings are intentionally above the level of your students' writing, they are not above their level of reading— if students are willing to stretch. If, at first, they understand only bits and pieces of a reading, they need not despair. They should still be encouraged to do some or all of the exercises and work through the process of their own writing. Breakthroughs in reading and writing ability come at different times for different students, and neither we nor they can predict when these small victories will occur.

Overall, the readings are there to exercise students' reading muscles, to serve as written input to the language acquisition process, and to challenge and stimulate students to share parallel ideas and experiences. In effect, the readings provide context and support for your students' writing. Don't expect their writing to be an imitation of the essays in the book, however; it will be additional writing, at a less sophisticated level, within the same thematic range. At first, it may amount to only a few simple lines. Be patient; it will develop!

The exercises that follow the readings in each unit are varied in order to maintain student interest, as well as to cover linguistic ground over the scope of the book. Many of the grammar exercises are designed to review structures that students may need to check as they edit their work. The exercises can be deleted or supplemented, depending on what your students need to work on.

THE LESSONS: WRITING

The process that students follow in writing their essays is just as important as the essays they write. Built into the process as taught in this book are strategies that will help students accomplish a number of important goals:

1. become more aware of the needs of their readers
2. generate ideas
3. get feedback throughout the writing process
4. expand their ideas and refine what they mean
5. revise and edit

Experience has shown that we can not assume that students have sophisticated rhetorical skills that can simply be transferred to English; as likely as not, many of them don't feel confident in writing their native language, while others have learned to write according to formulaic prescriptions. Either way, you may have to help students develop rhetorical skills that haven't been developed in any language.

Throughout this book I ask you to give attention to the writing process. However, students will surely want you to read their writing and assess it, and you may already have found satisfactory ways of responding to their writing. My own choice is to respond to the content of their essays and to select one rhetorical or grammatical problem to highlight and note on each essay. The pattern of student errors will indicate problems they are ready to attack next.

THE LESSONS: POSTWRITING

The postwriting activity at the end of each unit consists of an entry into a learning log. In this section, entitled "Winding Down," students are asked questions that direct their attention to language learning experiences and perhaps to their own anxiety and frustration. Although the questions do not need to be answered one by one, they are there to "prime the pump" and give students "permission" to participate in their own learning. The log is simply a sheet of notebook paper that students write their thoughts on and turn in at the end of each unit.

I suggest that you respond to students' logs by writing several comments in return on their papers—commiserating with a problem, sharing the joy of an important discovery, answering a question, or sharing a similar insight or experience. (At all costs, I urge you to resist the urge to correct students' logs; simply respond as a reader.) In addition, you might handwrite a collective log to the class, making a copy for each student. In my log to the class, I comment on our recent work, cite the ideas or comments of a classmate, and summarize some of the content of their individual logs. I've found that students dearly love to see themselves cited or quoted in my log!

The purpose of the learning log is threefold: to give students a reason to reflect on the learning process, set up another writing situation with a real reader, and help provide a sense of collaboration between you and your students. Writing a learning log can be as valuable as writing a journal or an essay. In different ways, each enhances a writing program and promotes writing development.

TOPICS AND RHETORIC

In content, the units focus on aspects of daily life that touch us all—families, special occasions, favorite and familiar places, trips, unusual experiences. These topics are so universal that they can easily be personalized by your students, a factor that will make writing easier and more meaningful. None of us can write well on topics that are remote to our personal knowledge and experience.

Rhetorically, the readings and students' parallel writing are narrative in Units 3, 4, 6, 7, 9, and 10 and descriptive in Units 1, 2, 5, and 8. You may wish to point out that in writing it is the content and the writers' intentions that lead the way, not a particular rhetorical mode.

In my guidelines to the student writers whose essays appear in the readings, I asked them to explore certain topics without giving them rhetorical specifications. The rhetorical "shape" that each essay took was determined by what the writer wanted to say about a particular topic. Such is the nature of written language.

ORGANIZATION AND GRAMMAR

In organization, the readings illustrate the following:

> Chronological order (a time arrangement): Units 3, 4, 6, 9, 10
> Spatial order (a space arrangement): Units 5, 8
> Enumeration (a listing of information): Units 1, 2
> Shift of conversational subject (movement from one topic to
> another): Unit 7

Again, students with strong rhetorical backgrounds may be interested in some of the more academic and analytic aspects of English discourse as they become more proficient in the language. And they may want to know some terminology and rhetorical concepts. If they are curious, diagrams are a good visual way of explaining organizational arrangements:

Chronological order:

1
2
3

time

Example: morning, afternoon, evening

Spatial order: a.   b.

| x | x |

| x |
| x |
| x |

Example: front, center, back

Enumeration: ◯ = ☐, ☐, ☐

Example: John = male, oldest child, student

Shift of subject:

Example: I, you, your brother

Whenever direct attention is given to rhetorical analysis, it should be emphasized that writers do not set out, for example, to spatially order their content; spatial order of details will emerge when a writer wants the reader to "see" how something or someone looks. It is the by-product of a writer acting on intentions.

It is up to you to determine when attending to rhetorical matters is confusing or when it satisfies the intellectual curiosity of academically minded adults. A lot of rhetorical know-how is acquired by students without their conscious knowledge of it. They simply put it into practice. It is my sense that at the beginning levels of ESL writing, such rhetorical matters are part of "teacher knowledge."

Structurally, the content of the readings is developed within the time frames of present and past. Accordingly, the writers have used primarily the simple present, present continuous, or simple past tenses. (The past continuous and perfect tenses pop up occasionally, but are never focused on.)

The progression of tenses through the ten units is largely the result of the arrangement of topic areas, rather than a rigid editing of the readings. For example, the topics that make use of the simple past tense are placed toward the end of the book, since present grammar tenses are traditionally introduced before the many irregular past forms.

Although this traditional arrangement is based more on custom than logic, I have chosen to follow that tradition. This is not to say that students should be exposed only to language forms that we think they are ready for. In fact, it is often productive for them to work with content that is comprehensible, yet which contains structural forms that they may not be ready to produce. Working with such forms, even if outside the level of conscious awareness, readies students for language that they may end up acquiring without any direct work on their part or yours. This is language development at its best.

Overall, you will see a grading of length and structural complexity of the readings according to what classroom experience has shown is manageable. Note that this is done as naturally as possible without affecting the authenticity of the readings, with forms appearing in the readings before they become the grammatical focus of a particular unit. The result may be that students try to use a form before it becomes part of a lesson; so much the better. There is never a wrong time for students to be curious about their new language.

A SUGGESTED TIME FRAME FOR THE LESSONS

Each unit is designed to provide five to six hours of classwork. If students meet for composition five days a week, as they do in some intensive ESL programs, much of the basic work can be done in class. If they meet less often, more will need to be assigned as homework in order to complete a unit in a week's time. If you prefer a less rigorous pace, stretch each unit over a week and a half.

What follows is a six-day suggested plan for each unit:

Day 1: Prewriting and prereading. Students write in their journals and play with words in class. Then they prepare for the reading, by combining individual work with oral sharing. If time permits, present the readings by "telling" them while students follow along with the illustrations. Homework assignment: Have students study the readings, looking up and writing down new vocabulary. (Urge them to keep a special vocabulary notebook.)

Day 2: Readings and exercises. Several students retell the readings, while others listen and follow the illustrations to see if anything has been left out. The listeners then offer corrections or supplementary information. Alternative plans are for you to ask questions whose answers, in effect, constitute a retelling of the readings or to write sequential questions on the board and have students respond orally. Next, have students refer to their own questions from the prereading and comment on any similarities or discrepancies between what they expected and what they actually found. If possible, do some or all of the exercises that follow the readings. They can be done individually or collectively. Homework assignment: Have students complete any unfinished exercises.

Day 3: Collaborative work and decisions about reader needs. Begin by checking exercises that weren't checked on Day 2. Then proceed to the first two steps of "Parallel Writing" for their own writing. (In Units 1 through 8, students work with partners; in Units 9 and 10, they work in larger groups.) After students decide on a reader, have them verbalize the answers to the questions. Perhaps a random check of the class will do. Homework assignment: Have students follow the third step of the instructions (draft an essay).

Day 4: More collaborative work and revising. Any general problems that emerge as students work on their writing can be addressed at the beginning of class. Have students work with their partners again (step 4) and then go on to step 5, checking back to the readings and revising their drafts. Homework assignment: Have students finish the revised draft.

Day 5: Reader response. Readers read the essays given to them and respond in writing (step 6). Writers get a chance to ask their readers for clarification, if needed. Then, based on the readers' comments, writers revise their drafts. Depending upon how much time is needed for exchanging comments, this last redrafting may be completed in part or entirely at home.

Day 6: Wrap up. Students write in their learning logs in class and turn them in to you. At this point, you may also want to collect the students' drafts. If the paper load is excessive, you might stagger your collection so that you don't see every student's drafts every week. Another option is to have students select which of every three or four series of drafts they want you to read and respond to. However you arrange it, I suggest that you not collect any work until after the third draft, when writers have had a chance to act on their readers' comments. Your comments and evaluation will thereby take into account the quality of the final draft as well as the writer's increasing ability to revise from one draft to the next.

SOME NOTES ON THE WRITING PROCESS

Built into each unit of this book is a process within a process. The larger process takes your class from journal writing ("Warming Up") to log writing ("Winding Down"); the smaller one takes your students from talking to a partner about ideas for writing to writing an essay ("Parallel Writing").

The real focus, of course, is the writing process itself which underlies and subsumes the other two. While we are continually learning more about the writing process, what we know so far is that it involves a lot of thinking and generating of ideas (called the "invention" stage by some theorists) and a lot of drafting and reclarifying. And we know that redrafting can be further refined into stages of revision, editing and proofreading.

The writing process also appears to be more cyclical than linear. For instance, writers may still be coming up with new ideas when they are already into the revision stage.

Research seems to indicate that writers become more successful when they understand that their ideas emerge over the course of thinking, reading, talking and writing about a topic; that their ideas do not arrive in a neat package, a gift of the gods.

Research also suggests that writers become more successful when they are not overly concerned with correctness in the early stages of their writing. They need to allow themselves time to figure out what they want to say before worrying about grammar and mechanics. Successful writers seem to leave the "cleaning up" for the editing and final proofreading stages.

Many of these aspects of the writing process will be readily apparent as your students work through each unit of the book. In particular, students will be generating ideas as they write in their journals, play with words, anticipate the content of the readings, read, work with their writing partners, anticipate their readers' needs, and draft their essays.

If your students still need additional activities to generate creative thinking and writing, have them try these:

1. Brainstorm a topic by listing all/any possible points to be covered.
2. List any words possibly related to the topic.
3. Draw pictures (stick figures permitted!) related to the topic.
4. Make a list of points that you would like to read about in someone else's essay on the topic.
5. Write the last (first) sentence of an essay on the topic.
6. Describe your most vivid memory or experience related to any aspect of the topic.

As you work through each unit of this book, you will see that students are drafting at almost every step along the way, even before they are given instructions for essay writing. They are drafting as well as generating ideas when they write in their journals; ideas expressed there will likely find their way into students' essays.

Once students see that their writing parallels the readings, they will probably start to compose in their heads as they read—trying out new combinations of words to fit with their own experiences and ideas. Further, students compose orally as they talk through their ideas with their writing partners; they continue to draft in response to the feedback from their partners as well as to their readers' anticipated needs.

As your students draft in response to feedback from their partners' and readers', they are, of course, already revising. By revising, I mean adjusting the content. In other words, they may need to explain in greater detail or more precise language something that is unclear; they might fill in pieces of information that are in their heads but are apparently unexpressed to the partner and/or the reader; or they may begin to take out pieces that they find irrelevant. The process of revising may be very uneven at first; your students may be wedded to what they have written and the partners and readers may be reluctant to actively participate or may simply think that everything is okay. Give them time; it often takes several weeks.

If your students require additional strategies to help them revise, have them try these:

1. Outline what they have written; an outline will pinpoint where the development of ideas breaks down.
2. Have a classmate outline what they have written; the gaps will be apparent.
3. Read their writing to themselves, alone and out loud; sometimes reading aloud helps writers gain some distance from their writing.
4. Type their writing or put it on a word processor; sometimes a change in visual appearance will create the distance a writer needs for revision.
5. Rewrite what they think they have written; writers may actually "find" what they were trying to get at all along.

Some of your students may edit their work too soon and end up with underdeveloped content; others may not edit at all and turn in work that is "sloppy." Either way, your students will benefit from a definable editing/proofing stage, when everyone becomes accustomed to checking and correcting as a matter of course.

Reading a paper for a final "clean up" needs to occur at the end of a final drafting—before the writing is "published" or evaluated. You may have students work from a checklist of problem items to be located and examined; some students work well from simple holistic reading, where they concentrate more on form than content; others need the extra support of having the teacher mark/circle/ underline what they have missed and need to correct. Whichever method you choose to direct their attention to problems that they have the ability to spot, they need to eventually become their own editors.

EXPECTATIONS AND CONCLUSION

At the end of the term, you may want to prepare a table of contents for a special composition notebook that each student provides and keeps, a notebook containing all of the student's numbered and dated compositions for the course. Reader responses and learning logs might be included as well. The notebook can serve as a handy reference and a valuable resource for future composition work.

If resources permit, you might ask each student to select a favorite piece of writing for "publication" and then make copies for everyone in the class. That way, each student could finish the course with a "class book" (actually a binder of some sort) that contains a piece of writing by every member of the class. You might include one yourself! This is a good way to remember everyone.

After working through all the lessons in the book, students can be expected to write a one-to-two-page essay on a familiar, everyday topic. You can expect the essay to be coherent and reasonably accurate.

What is more important than any external standard are the changes evident in a student's writing over the weeks of the term. In order to document how dramatic these changes may well be, you might want to ask students to write a spontaneous essay in class—perhaps autobiographical in nature—at the beginning of the term; then repeat the assignment near the end, without there having been any response to the first assignment or any direct preparation for the second. (You can simply tell students that you are saving their first assignment for later.) You will be amazed at the tangible differences, differences that you may not have been aware of as you worked with students on a day-to-day basis.

Best of luck as you begin the term!

TO THE STUDENT

Welcome to *Idea Exchange, Book 1*, and to the world of English! In this book, you will practice reading, writing, and speaking English. You will meet four people as you work through the lessons. They are students like you. Their names are Hassen, Lien, Sebastian, and Cherry. Hassen is a student from Tunisia; his first language is Arabic. Lien is a student from Taiwan; her first language is Chinese. Sebastian is a student from Honduras; his first language is Spanish. Cherry is a native speaker of English, and she is from Louisiana.

All four study at the University of New Orleans in New Orleans, Louisiana. If you don't know New Orleans, it is an old American city on the Mississippi River, near the Gulf of Mexico. It is a city with a long history. Before it was American, it was Spanish and then French. It became a city in the year 1718.

You will use English to learn more about New Orleans. You will also learn more about Hassen, Lien, Sebastian, and Cherry. You will learn about Tunisia, Taiwan, Honduras, and Louisiana. You will use English to tell others about yourself and your background. Good luck with your English! I hope that you will enjoy this book! The information below will help you as you begin your work.

Writers need tools and materials, just like painters. You will need these:

1. a notebook for your journal writing
2. 8½ × 11 inch loose-leaf notebook paper for your essays and your learning log
3. pens and pencils
4. a good translation dictionary and a simplified English–English dictionary.

As you read the writing by Hassen, Lien, Sebastian, and Cherry, please follow these rules:

1. Read it all before you go to your dictionary.
2. Read groups of words; do not stop after every word.
3. Read with your eyes; do not move your lips.
4. Use your dictionary after you finish reading. Then read again.
5. Look for important connections between ideas. These words show connections: *and, example, because, after, while, first, finally*, etc.

   Your attitude about writing is important. Here are some points to keep in mind:

1. Nobody's writing is perfect.
2. Writing is hard work in any language.
3. We know that you are an intelligent person, even if your English is simple and imperfect. Be patient with yourself! Be patient with us!
4. You need to read English in order to write English.
5. You need to think in order to write.
6. The point of writing is to express your ideas.

How is your attitude?

   Here are some basic rules for writing. Come back to them from time to time. They will help you arrange, punctuate, and capitalize your words:

1. Leave margins.
2. Indent each paragraph.
3. Put a period at the end of each sentence; put a question mark at the end of each question.
   Example: John is absent today.
             Is he sick?
4. Use capital letters correctly:
   a. names of people
      Example: Peter Andres

   b. names of cities
      Example: Paris

   c. names of countries
      Example: Japan

   d. names of rivers
      Example: the Amazon River

   e. names of streets
      Example: Michigan Avenue

   f. names of buildings
      Example: the Empire State Building

g. names of organizations
   Example: the United Nations

h. names of national, ethnic, and racial groups
   Example: French, Jewish, Hispanic

i. titles
   Example: Dr. Santini

j. the first person singular pronoun: I

k. days of the week
   Example: Thursday

l. months of the year
   Example: April

m. holidays
   Example: Christmas

n. titles of books, magazines, newspapers
   Example: the New York Times

o. the first letter at the beginning of each sentence and question
   Example: Are you happy?

Placement of parts of an essay:

Your name

Title of your composition

XXXXXXXXXXXXXXXXXXXXXXXXXXXX. XXXXXXX
XXXXXXXXXXXXXXXXXXXXXXXX. XXXXXXXXXXXX
XXXXXXXXXXXXXXXXXXXXXXXXXXXXX. XXXX
XXXXXXXXXXXXXXXXXXXXXXXX. XXXXXXXXXX
XXXXXXXXXXXXXXXXXXXXXXXXXXXXXXXXXXX.
XXXXXXXXXXXXXXXXXXXXXXXXXXX. XXXXXX
XXXXXXXXXXXX. XXXXXXXXXXXXXXXXXXXX
XXXXXXXXXXXXXXXXX.

XXXXXXXXXXXXXXXXXXXXXXXXXXXXXXXXX
XXXXXXXXXX. XXXXXXXXXXXXXXXXXXXXXXX.
XXXXXXXXXXXXXXXXXXXXX. XXXXXXXXXXXX
XXXXXXXXXXXX. XXXXXXXXXXXXXXXXXXXXX
XXXXXXXXXXXXXXXX. XXXXXXXXXXXXXXXX
XXXXXXXXXXXXXXXX. XXXXXXXXXXXXXX
XXXXXXXXXXXXX. XXXXXXXXXXXXXXXXXXX
XXXXXXXXXXXXXXXXXXXXX. XXXXXXXXXX
XXXXXXXXXX. XXXXXXXXXXXXXXXXXXXXXXX.
XXXXXXXXXXXXXXXXXXXXX. XXXXXXXXXX
XXXXXXXXXXXX. XXXXXXXXXXXXXXXXXXXXX
XXXXXXXXXXXXXXXXXX.

XXXXXXXXXXXXXXXXXXXXXXXX. XXXXXX
XXXXXXXXXXXXXXXX. XXXXXXXXXXXXXXXX
XXXXXXXXXXXXXXXXXXXX. XXXXXXXXXX
XXXXXXXXXXXXXXXXXXXXXXXXXXXXXXX
XXXXXXXXXXXXX.

left margin   ☐ indentation   right margin

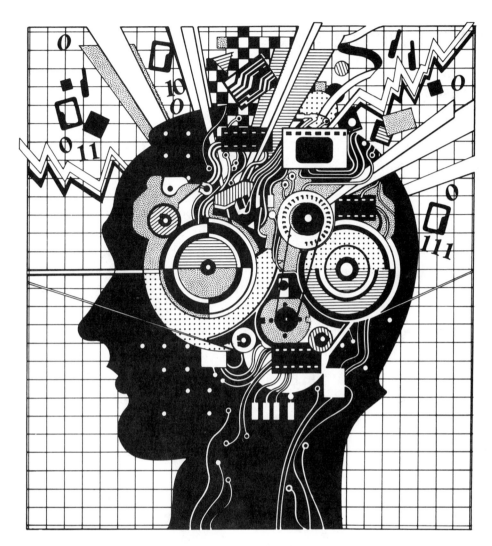

UNIT 1

INDIVIDUALS

Rhetorical Focus: Description

Organizational Focus: Enumeration

Grammatical Focus: Simple Present Tense Review (*be*)

Warming Up

YOUR JOURNAL

Write in your journal for five minutes. Write about yourself. Answer this question:

> Who are you?

(Remember that you are the only one who will see this journal.) Write words. Write sentences. Write anything that comes to mind. Don't worry about correct grammar. Just keep writing. If you can't think of anything, write "I don't know what to write about myself." Write it again until something comes to mind.

PLAYING WITH WORDS

In this section, you can have some fun with words and writing. Read the directions and let your mind wander. (Write the words in your journal.)

1. Write five words about *people*.
   Example: busy
              tall
2. Write five words about *cars*.
   Example: fast
              expensive
3. Write five words about *trees*.
   Example: tall
              shady

Share your words with your classmates.

GETTING READY TO READ

The essays in this unit are by two students. Their names are Hassen and Lien. Hassen is from Tunisia. Lien is from Taiwan. They are writing about themselves. You are the reader. What do you want to know about them?

1. Write questions that you want them to answer about themselves.

      Example: How old are you?

2. Write words that you expect them to use in their essays.

      Example: school
                      study

Share your questions and words with your classmates.

Reading 1A

Please read about Lien:

ABOUT ME

My name is Ruo Lien. My name means "lotus" in Chinese. A lotus is a beautiful flower. In the Chinese culture, the lotus is a symbol of purity. My parents want me to be good, pure, and beautiful. That is why they named me Ruo Lien.

I try hard to be a good person, but it is difficult. I help poor people. I help old people, too. I try hard to be honest. I always tell the truth. I study hard. I study art, and I want to be a good artist.

Am I beautiful? Well, I am beautiful in my parents' eyes. That is important to me.

Reading 1B

Please read about Hassen:

MYSELF

My name is Hassen. I am twenty-seven years old. I am male. I am from Tunisia, but I am a student in the United States. I am single now, but I hope to marry one day.

I come from a large family. I have a mother, father, four brothers, and three sisters. They are in Tunisia. I love my family very much. I miss them. It is difficult for me to be far away from my home.

I am a shy person, but I like to laugh. I like to be with children. Children are important in my life. At home, I play with my sister's children. I also like the sea. At home, I go out in my father's boat. He is a fisherman. I like the sound of the sea. It is my favorite music. I also like to cook. My mother says that I am a good cook. Finally, I like to work with wood. I make toys for children out of wood.

Exercises on the Readings

EXERCISE A: COMPREHENSION

Please circle the letters below to show the correct answers. The information comes from Lien's and Hassen's essays in this unit. If you don't know an answer, go back to their essays.

1. In Chinese, Lien's name means
   a. "flower."
   b. "rose."
   c. "lotus."

2. A lotus is
   a. a beautiful flower.
   b. a pure person.
   c. a good artist.

3. In Lien's culture, the lotus is a symbol of
   a. art.
   b. purity.
   c. beauty.

4. Lien's parents want her to be
   a. good, pure, and beautiful.
   b. poor, old, and important.
   c. Chinese, difficult, and shy.

5. Lien knows that she is beautiful
   a. in her friends' eyes.
   b. in her boyfriend's eyes.
   c. in her parents' eyes.

6. Hassen is
   a. twenty-six years old.
   b. twenty-seven years old.
   c. twenty-eight years old.

7. Hassen is
   a. a fisherman.
   b. a student.
   c. a cook.

8. Hassen is
   a. single.
   b. married.
   c. divorced.

9. Hassen likes to
   a. be away from his family and have a good time.
   b. laugh, be with children, and play football.
   c. laugh, cook, and work with wood.

10. Hassen's mother says that
    a. she loves her son.
    b. her son is a good cook.
    c. she likes to cook.

EXERCISE B: SIMPLE PRESENT TENSE

Part 1. Please write *is* or *are* in the empty spaces.

Lien's full name _____ Ruo Lien. The meaning of her name _____ "lotus." A lotus _____ a beautiful flower. In the Chinese culture, the lotus _____ a symbol of purity. Lien knows that she _____ pure and beautiful in her parents' eyes.

Lien's friend, Hassen, _____ from Tunisia. He _____ twenty-seven years old. He _____ a student, too. His parents _____ in Tunisia, and he misses them very much. His older sister _____ the mother of three children. Hassen _____ a good uncle. He likes to be with his nieces and nephew. Children _____ important in his life.

Part 2. Please answer the questions below in complete sentences.

Example: What is Lien's full name?
Her full name is Ruo Lien.
or
It is Ruo Lien.

1. What is the meaning of Lien's name?

_____

2. What is a lotus?

_____

3. What is the lotus a symbol of?

_____

4. How old is Hassen?

_____

5. Where is he from?

_____

6. Where is his family?

_____

7. What is Hassen?

_____

8. What is his father?

_____

9. What is his favorite music?

_____

10. What are his interests?

_____

EXERCISE C: WORDWORK

Please complete each sentence with a word from the list below:

pure	culture
single	children
favorite	eyes
male	symbol
meanings	means

1. In some languages, names have _____ .
2. In Chinese, the name Ruo Lien _____ "lotus."
3. In the Chinese _____ , the lotus is a symbol of purity.
4. In all cultures, a red cross is a _____ of medical aid.
5. The word "purity" is the noun form of the word " _____ ."

6. Children are always beautiful in their parents' _____ .

7. Hassen is not a female. He is a _____ .

8. Hassen is not married. He is _____ .

9. Hassen does not have a child, but _____ are important to him.

10. Hassen likes the sound of the sea best of all. It is his _____ music.

Parallel Writing

You have read about Lien and Hassen. Now you are ready to write about yourself. This is your topic: yourself. Your writing will be "parallel" to Lien's and Hassen's. This means you will write about the same topic, but not in exactly the same way. Your essay will probably be shorter and simpler than theirs. Follow these instructions.

TALK WITH A PARTNER

1. Choose a partner (or your teacher may choose one for you). You and your partner will help each other write. But first, tell your partner about yourself. Use sentences like these:

My name is _____ .
I come from _____ .
Now I'm living in _____ .
In my free time, I like to _____ .

Your partner will take notes (write down only the important information). He or she will probably ask you questions ("How do you spell that?" "Could you say that again, please?"). After you finish talking, ask your partner to read the information back to you. He or she will say:

Your name is _____ .
You come from _____ .
Now you're living in _____ .
In your free time, you like to _____ .

Did your partner understand everything? If not, tell him or her the correct information.

2. Now it's your partner's turn. Listen to your partner talk about himself or herself. Take notes. Then read your notes back to your partner. Did you understand everything? If not, your partner will help you write the correct information.

Now you and your partner know each other a little better.

MAKE SOME DECISIONS

Before you write your essay, you need to make some decisions:

Who is your reader? (Whenever you write, you need to think about your reader. For this unit, choose a classmate, but not your partner. Your teacher may help you choose a reader. Later, you and your classmate will exchange papers.)

What does your reader want to know about you? What questions do you think he or she wants you to answer? (Think about what you and your partner talked about.) Write down questions like these:

What is your name?
What country are you from?
Where are you living now?
What language do you speak?

WRITE A DRAFT

Write a draft of an essay about yourself. A draft is one of several versions of an essay. It is not the final essay. In your draft, answer the questions that you wrote, but don't write the questions. Write your sentences in paragraph form. (Look at Lien's and Hassen's essays for examples of paragraph form). As you write, you may get more ideas. Add these ideas to your draft.

READ ALOUD TO YOUR PARTNER

1. Read your draft aloud to your partner (not your reader). Your partner should listen carefully and think about these questions:

Is the information clear?
Is something not clear?
What else do I want to know?

Your partner may make comments while you read. He or she may say "Excuse me, I didn't understand that." If your partner says that an idea is not clear, write it in a different way. Your partner may make other comments after you finish reading. The purpose of these comments is to help you write better, not to say what is right and what is wrong.

2. Now ask your partner to read your draft to you. Do you like what you hear? Does the draft say what you want to say?

3. Now change roles with your partner. Listen to your partner's draft. Talk about it together. Then read the draft aloud to your partner.

WRITE A SECOND DRAFT

Rework your draft. Rework means to write it again with changes. All writers need to rework their writing. No piece of writing is ever really finished. As you write, you may get new ideas. Include them. Look at Hassen's and Lien's essays. They may give you ideas that you can add.

EXCHANGE DRAFTS WITH YOUR READER

When you feel that your new draft is finished, give it to your reader. Your reader will give you his or her draft. You should read each other's drafts and write on them. Write comments like:

> I understand this part.
> I don't understand this.
> This is very interesting.
> I want to know more about this.

You may want to know more information. You should write questions, such as:

> What street do you live on?
> Do you speak any other languages?

REWRITE YOUR DRAFT

Look at your essay and your reader's comments carefully. Rewrite your essay one more time. Your teacher may want to read the drafts and the final essay. Save this final essay and your drafts in your notebook.

Winding Down

Write a few lines in your learning log. Your learning log is a way for you to write to your teacher. Your teacher is the reader of your log. For this unit, write to him or her about these questions:

Do you like to write in your native language?
Do you like to write in English?
Did you like writing about yourself?
Did you like reading your partner's writing?

Write as much about these questions as you want. Or write about other things that you want your teacher to know. Give your paper to your teacher. He or she will read it, write some comments, and then return it to you to keep in your log.

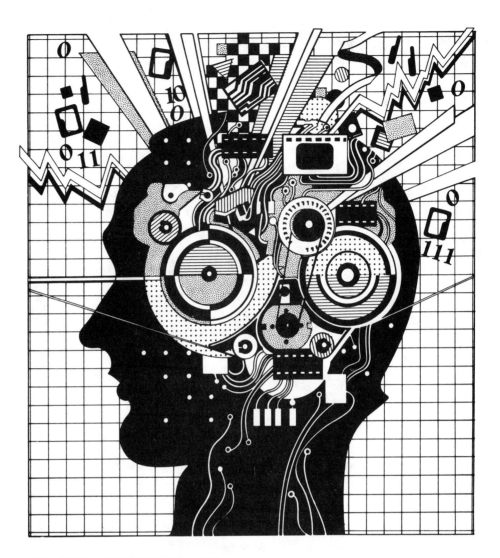

UNIT 2

FAMILIES

Rhetorical Focus: Description

Organizational Focus: Enumeration

Grammatical Focus: Simple Present Tense Review (All Verbs)

Warming Up

YOUR JOURNAL

Write in your journal for five minutes. In the last unit you wrote about yourself. Now write about your family. Answer questions such as these:

> Who are your family members?
> How old are they?
> Where do they live?
> Do you see each other often?

Write words or sentences. Don't worry about correct grammar. Just keep writing. If you can't think of anything, write "I don't know what to write about my family." Write it again until something comes to mind.

PLAYING WITH WORDS

1. Think of a *famous person* and write down three things you know about *that person's family*.

    Example: John F. Kennedy.
                      He had two children.

2. Write down some *animals* that you know and the words for their *children*.

    Example: cat–kitten

Share your ideas and words with your classmates.

GETTING READY TO READ

The essays in this unit are by two students. Their names are Lien and Sebastian. You know Lien from Unit 1. You don't know Sebastian. He is from Honduras. They are writing about their families. What do you want to know about them?

1. Write questions that you want them to answer about their families.

    Example: How large is your family?

2. Write words that you expect them to use in their essays.
      Example: mother
                   brother

Share your questions and words with your classmates.

Reading 2A

Please read about Lien's family:

MY FAMILY

There are six people in my family: my grandmother, my parents, my older sister, my younger brother, and I. We are from Taiwan, but we live in New Orleans now. We are very close. In the Chinese culture, children live with their parents for a long time. Daughters live with their parents until they get married. After the children are married, parents live with their oldest son. My parents have only one son. They will live with him.

In Taiwan, my father was a sea captain. Now he works in a Chinese restaurant. My mother was a teacher. She doesn't speak enough English to teach in the United States. Now she is a seamstress. My sister, my brother, and I are students. I am an art student at the University of New Orleans. My sister is a business student at the same school. My brother studies biochemistry at Tulane University. My grandmother stays at home. She cooks for us and takes care of the house.

Reading 2B

Please read about Sebastian's family:

MY FAMILY

There are five people in my family: my mother, my sister, my brother-in-law, my twin brother, and I. My father is dead. He died in Honduras six years ago. We live in New Orleans now, and we are a close family.

My mother, Rosamalia, works for the Honduran government. She is the Consul of Honduras in New Orleans. She likes New Orleans very much. She is proud that there are many Hondurans in New Orleans. My sister, Mayra, works in a hotel. She is an assistant manager of the Hyatt Hotel in New Orleans. My sister wants to own a hotel one day. She likes to work with people, and she is also an excellent cook. My brother-in-law, Hector, is a building inspector for the city of New Orleans. He loves to play soccer. My brother, Miguel, is a student at the University of New Orleans. I am a student there, too. He works in a seafood restaurant at night. He is a waiter. He likes to travel. He wants to be a businessman and own his own company.

We are a busy family. We study or work every day, but we always have time for each other.

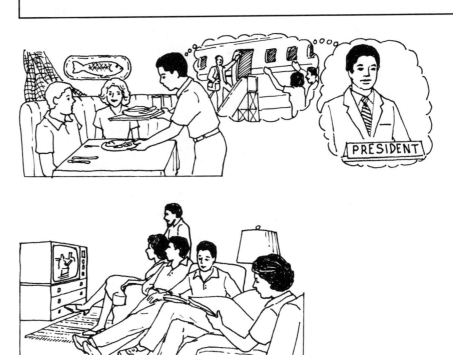

Exercises on the Readings

EXERCISE A: COMPREHENSION

Please circle the letters below to show the correct answers. The information comes from Lien's and Sebastian's essays in this unit. If you don't know an answer, go back to their essays.

1. In Lien's family, there are
   a. five people.
   b. six people.
   c. seven people.

2. Lien has
   a. an older sister and a younger brother.
   b. two older sisters.
   c. an older brother and a younger sister.

3. In the Chinese culture, daughters live with their parents
   a. until they start college.
   b. until they get married.
   c. until they have children.

4. In the Chinese culture, parents live with
   a. their oldest daughter.
   b. their youngest child.
   c. their oldest son.

5. In Taiwan, Lien's mother was
   a. a teacher.
   b. a seamstress.
   c. a sea captain.

6. In Sebastian's family, there are
   a. four people.
   b. five people.
   c. six people.

7. Sebastian's mother works for
   a. the Hyatt Hotel.
   b. the University of New Orleans.
   c. the Honduran government.

8. Sebastian's sister works for
   a. the Hyatt Hotel.
   b. the Honduran government.
   c. the University of New Orleans.

9. Sebastian's brother-in-law is
   a. a consul.
   b. a building inspector.
   c. a cook.

10. Sebastian's brother is
    a. a cook and a hotel manager.
    b. a consul and a businessman.
    c. a student and a waiter.

EXERCISE B: SIMPLE PRESENT TENSE

Part 1. Please answer the questions below with complete sentences. Give the correct information about Lien's and Sebastian's families.

> Example: Does Lien's father work in a hotel?
> *No, he works in a Chinese restaurant.*

1. Does Lien's mother work as a waitress?

   _____

2. Does Lien study business?

   _____

3. Does Lien's sister study art?

   _____

4. Does Lien's brother teach biochemistry?

   _____

5. Does Lien's grandmother work?

   _____

6. Does Sebastian's mother work for the Mexican government?

   _____

7. Does Sebastian's sister study at the university?

   _____

8. Does Sebastian's brother own a seafood restaurant?

   _____

9. Does Sebastian's brother want to be a hotel manager?

_____

10. Does Sebastian's brother-in-law like to play cards?

_____

Part 2. Please answer the questions below with complete sentences. Use *There is* or *There are* in each sentence. In this kind of sentence, the subject follows the verb.

>   Example: What about hotels in New Orleans? Are there many?
>   *There are many hotels in New Orleans.*

1. What about Lien's family? Is it large? How many people?

_____

2. What about girls in her family? Any daughters?

_____

3. What about Sebastian's family? Is it large?

_____

4. What about boys in Sebastian's family? Any sons?

_____

5. What about Hondurans in New Orleans? How many?

_____

EXERCISE C: AGREEMENT

Please complete each sentence with a word from the list below. Pay attention to the subject (singular or plural) of each sentence.

live	study	has	work	want
lives	studies	have	works	wants

1. Lien _____ with her family in New Orleans.
2. Lien's father _____ in a Chinese restaurant.
3. Lien's parents _____ three children.
4. Lien _____ art at the University of New Orleans.
5. In the Chinese culture, parents _____ with their oldest son after their daughters marry.

6. Sebastian's brother _____ a job in a restaurant.

7. Sebastian and his brother both _____ at the University of New Orleans.

8. Sebastian's mother and sister both _____ outside the home.

9. Sebastian's brother, Miguel, _____ to be a businessman.

10. Sebastian and his brother both _____ to get degrees from the university.

Parallel Writing

You have read about Lien's and Sebastian's families. Now you are ready to write about your own family. Your writing will be "parallel" to Lien's and Sebastian's. In other words, you will write about the same topic (families), but not in exactly the same way. Your essay will probably be shorter and simpler than theirs. Follow these instructions.

TALK WITH A PARTNER

1. Choose a partner. (You may choose the same partner you did in Unit 1 or a different partner.) Tell your partner about your family. Include information such as the following:

- ☐ the number of people in your family
- ☐ where they live
- ☐ what they do for a living

Your partner will take notes. He or she will probably ask you questions. After you finish talking, ask your partner to read the notes back to you. Did he or she understand everything? If not, tell him or her the correct information.

2. Now it's your partner's turn. Listen to your partner talk about his or her family. Take notes. Then read your notes back to your partner. Did you understand everything? If not, your partner will help you with the correct information.

Now do you know something about your partner's family? Does your partner know something about yours?

MAKE SOME DECISIONS

Before you write your essay, you need to make these decisions:

Who is your reader? (Choose a different classmate each time.)

What does your reader want to know about your family? What questions do you think he or she wants you to answer? (Think about what you and your partner talked about.) Write down questions like these:

> How many people are in your family?
> Where do they live?
> What do they do for a living?
> Do you see them often?

WRITE A DRAFT

Write a draft of an essay about your family. Remember that a draft is not the final essay. Answer the questions that you wrote, but don't write the questions. Write your sentences in paragraph form. As you write, you may get more ideas. Add these ideas to your draft.

READ ALOUD TO YOUR PARTNER

1. Read your draft aloud to your partner (not your reader). Your partner should listen carefully and think about these questions:

> Is the information clear?
> Is something not clear?
> What else do I want to know?

Your partner may make comments while you read. If your partner says that an idea is not clear, write it in a different way. Your partner may make other comments after you finish reading. Remember that the purpose of these comments is to help you write better, not to say what is right and what is wrong.

2. Ask your partner to read your draft to you. Listen to it as a stranger might listen to it. Are the ideas clear? Is it interesting?

3. Now change roles with your partner. Listen to your partner's draft. Talk about it together. Then read the draft aloud to your partner.

WRITE A SECOND DRAFT

Rework your draft. Remember that no piece of writing is ever really finished. You may have some fresh ideas; add them to your draft. Look at Sebastian's and Lien's essays. Borrow words and structures if you want.

EXCHANGE DRAFTS WITH YOUR READER

When you feel that your new draft is finished, give it to your reader. Your reader will give you his or her draft. You should read each other's drafts and write on them. Write comments like:

> This is very clear.
> I don't understand this.
> Very interesting.
> I want to know more about him.

You may want to know more information. If you do, you should write questions, such as:

> Where does your brother work?
> When will you visit your family again?

REWRITE YOUR DRAFT

Look at your essay and your reader's comments carefully. Rewrite your essay one more time. Your teacher may want to read the drafts and the final essay. Save this final essay and your drafts in your notebook.

Winding Down

Write a few lines in your learning log. Write to your teacher. For this unit, write to him or her about these questions:

> Did you like writing about your family?
> Was it easier than writing about yourself?
> Did your reader understand your essay?
> Did you like working with a reader?

Write as much about these questions as you want. Or write about other things that you want your teacher to know. Give your paper to your teacher. He or she will read it, write some comments, and then return it to you to keep in your log.

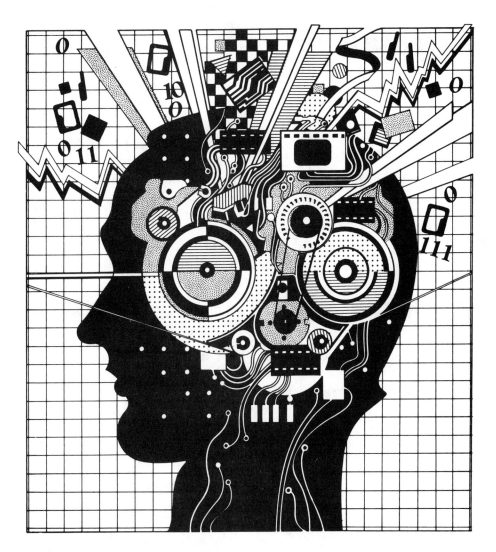

UNIT 3

ROUTINES

Rhetorical Focus: Narration

Organizational Focus: Chronological Order

Grammatical Focus: Frequency Word Review

Warming Up

YOUR JOURNAL

Write in your journal for five minutes. Write about a routine—something that you do regularly (every day, every other day, every Saturday, etc.). Some routine activities are exercising, doing housework, and going to work. Answer questions such as these:

> How often do you do your routine?
> Do you like to do it?
> Do you ever forget to do it?

Write words. Write sentences. Don't worry about correct grammar. Write what comes to mind. If you can't think of anything, write "I don't know what to write about a routine." Write it again until something comes to mind.

PLAYING WITH WORDS

1. Write a *silly* sentence about a routine activity.

    Example: I wash my pink elephant every Saturday.
2. Write a *serious* sentence about a routine activity.

    Example: He prays four times a day.

Share your ideas and words with your classmates.

GETTING READY TO READ

The essays in this unit are by Sebastian and Cherry. You know Sebastian from Unit 2. You don't know Cherry. Cherry is a North American; she was born in Louisiana. She is a student. They are writing about routines in their family life. You are the reader. What do you want to know about their routines?

1. Write questions that you want them to answer about their routines.

    Example: What time do you get up?

2. Write words that you expect them to use in their essays.

      Example: every (day, week, month, etc.)
                    evening

Share your words and questions with your classmates.

SUN	MON	TUE	WED	THUR	FRI	SAT
		1	2	3	4	5
6	7	8	9	10	11	12

Reading 3A

Please read about the Sunday routine in Sebastian's family:

SUNDAYS

Sunday is a very special day in my family. Sunday is the only day that we are at home together. On Sunday, we do many things together.

The day usually starts around eight o'clock in the morning. We wake up and have breakfast together. After breakfast, my mother usually starts cleaning the house. My sister goes to work in the garden. My brother-in-law cuts the grass, and my brother and I wash the cars. We finish our chores around 11:30 and get ready to go to church. Sunday mass starts at 12:30. We always go to church together.

After church, my sister starts cooking the Sunday meal. The Sunday meal is very important to us. We relax and talk about the week's events. We always eat Honduran food on Sunday. It is our family's tradition. After the Sunday meal, we sometimes go to a friend's house. Sometimes, friends come to our house. We talk, drink, and watch soccer on television. These visits often last two or three hours.

Sunday is always a family day. We do our work together, and we relax together. We are busy during the week, and Sunday is our time together.

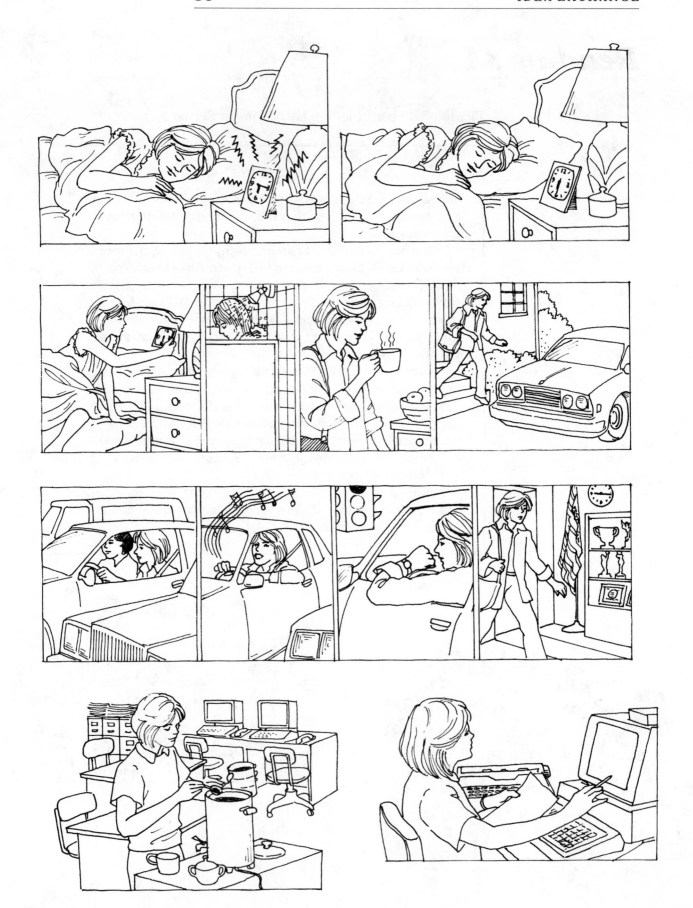

Reading 3B

Please read about Cherry's busy weekday routine:

THAT'S LIFE!

My weekday usually begins at 6:15 A.M. The alarm rings, and rings, and rings. Sometimes, I sleep until 6:30 anyway. During the next half-hour, I run from the shower to the kitchen and then to the car.

I always drive my mother to work. After I drop her off, I turn on the radio and listen to loud music. This helps me wake up. I usually sing when I hear my favorite songs. The other drivers sometimes give me strange looks. I usually hit every red light and arrive at school late.

I have a part-time job in the English Department at school. I am a student worker. My classes are usually later in the morning, and I work for a few hours before class. First, I open the office and prepare a pot of coffee. I make it for the teachers, but mainly I do it for myself! I watch the coffee to make it drip faster, but it never does. When it finally finishes, I pour myself a cup of coffee. I always make it strong and black. After I wake up a little more, I type or work at the computer until it is time for class. I am usually in class from 11:00 to 3:00.

Three afternoons a week, I go to another job. I work at a local hospital. I file medical records. When I work at the hospital, I get home at 11:00 at night. I am too tired to study then, and I go straight to bed. On my afternoons off, I study in the library at school. I sometimes fall asleep over my books. I need more time to study and sleep, but I don't have it. Who does? I guess that's life!

Exercises on the Readings

EXERCISE A: COMPREHENSION

Please circle the letters below to show the correct answers. The information comes from Sebastian's and Cherry's essays in this unit. If you don't know an answer, look back at their essays.

1. Sebastian's Sundays usually start at about
    a. seven o'clock.
    b. eight o'clock.
    c. nine o'clock.

2. Sebastian has breakfast with
    a. his mother and brother.
    b. his mother, brother, and sister.
    c. his mother, brother, sister, and brother-in-law.

3. On Sunday morning, Sebastian and his brother
    a. work in the garden.
    b. cut the grass.
    c. wash their cars.

4. After their chores, the family
    a. goes to church.
    b. eats the Sunday meal.
    c. visits with friends.

5. It is the family's tradition to
    a. watch soccer on television.
    b. eat Honduran food on Sunday.
    c. do their chores together.

6. On weekdays, Cherry's alarm rings at
    a. a quarter past six.
    b. six-thirty.
    c. a quarter to seven.

7. Loud music
    a. helps Cherry wake up.

    b. makes Cherry happy.

    c. gets attention from other drivers.

8. Cherry works part-time

    a. only in the English Department at her school.

    b. only at a local hospital.

    c. in the English Department at her school and at a local hospital.

9. Cherry drinks her coffee

    a. with milk.

    b. with milk and sugar.

    c. strong and black.

10. Cherry studies

    a. when she gets home from work.

    b. before class.

    c. on her afternoons off.

EXERCISE B: FREQUENCY WORDS

Please rewrite each sentence below. Add the word in parentheses to your sentence. Each word in parentheses tells generally how often the activity takes place. (Watch out. The word order with the verb *be* is different.)

    Example: Sebastian's Sundays start around 8:00 A.M. (usually)
                  Sebastian's Sundays usually start around 8:00 A.M.

1. Sebastian's family has breakfast together on Sunday. (always)

_____

2. After breakfast, his mother cleans the house. (usually)

_____

3. After chores, the family goes to church. (always)

_____

4. After the noonday meal, the family goes visiting. (sometimes)

_____

5. Their visits last two or three hours. (often)

_____

6. On weekdays, Cherry sleeps until 6:30. (sometimes)

_____

7. Cherry drives her mother to work. (always)

_____

8. Cherry is late for school. (usually)

_____

9. Cherry gets enough sleep. (rarely)

_____

10. Cherry has enough time to study. (never)

_____

EXERCISE C: CHRONOLOGICAL ORDER

Please put these sentences into the proper order. The order is according to time.

1. About 12:00, they get ready for church.
2. Then they have a pleasant breakfast together.
3. On Sundays, Sebastian's family wakes up around 8:00 A.M.
4. After breakfast, they do their chores.

The correct order is _____ , _____ , _____ , and _____ .

1. Later in the afternoon, they visit with friends.
2. Sunday mass starts at 12:30.
3. She always cooks Honduran food.
4. After church, Sebastian's sister prepares the Sunday meal.

The correct order is _____ , _____ , _____ , and _____ .

1. Cherry's weekdays begin early.
2. Then she runs from the shower to the kitchen to the car.
3. On her way to school, she drops her mother off at work.
4. She gets up around 6:15.

The correct order is _____ , _____ , _____ , and _____ .

1. She leaves the office to go to class at about 10:45.
2. Then she drinks some coffee before she starts typing.
3. Cherry works in the English Department office before class.
4. First, she opens the office and prepares a pot of coffee.

The correct order is _____ , _____ , _____ , and _____ .

1. There she files medical records.
2. When she gets home, she goes straight to bed.
3. She gets off work at 11:00 P.M.
4. Three afternoons a week, Cherry works at a hospital.

The correct order is _____ , _____ , _____ , and _____ .

Parallel Writing

Now that you have read about Cherry and Sebastian, you are probably ready to write about yourself and one of your routines. Remember that your essay will be parallel to Lien's and Sebastian's, but it will probably be shorter and simpler than theirs. Follow these instructions.

TALK WITH A PARTNER

1. Choose a partner. (You may choose the same partner you did in the last unit or a different partner.) Tell your partner about what you do every day—your daily routine. Or tell about something else that you do regularly. Include information such as:

☐ the parts of your routine (what you do first, second, etc.)
☐ how important this routine is to you
☐ if you like the routine

Your partner will take notes. After you finish talking, ask your partner to read the notes back to you. Did he or she understand everything? Tell your partner if some information is incorrect. Tell him or her the correct information.

2. Now it's your partner's turn. Listen to your partner talk about his or her routine. Take notes. Then read your notes back to your partner. Did you understand everything? If not, your partner will help you write the correct information.

Now you know something about another person's routine. Is it very different from yours?

MAKE SOME DECISIONS

Before you write your essay, you need to make these decisions:

Who is your reader? (Choose a different classmate each time.)

What does your reader want to know about your routine? What questions do you think he or she wants you to answer? (Think about what you and your partner talked about and write down some questions.)

WRITE A DRAFT

Write a draft of an essay about one of your routines. Remember that a draft is not the final essay. Answer the questions that you wrote, but don't write the questions. Write your sentences in paragraph form. As you write, you may get more ideas. Add these ideas to your draft.

READ ALOUD TO YOUR PARTNER

1. Read your draft aloud to your partner (not your reader). Your partner should listen carefully and think about these questions:

> Is the information clear?
> Is something not clear?
> What else do I want to know?

Your partner will probably make comments while you read. If your partner says that an idea is not clear, write it in a different way. Your partner may make other comments after you finish reading. Remember that the purpose of these comments is to help you write better, not to say what is right and what is wrong.

2. Ask your partner to read your draft to you. Listen to it as a stranger might listen to it. Are the ideas clear? Is it interesting?

3. Now change roles with your partner. Listen to your partner's draft. Talk about it together. Then read the draft aloud to your partner.

WRITE A SECOND DRAFT

Rework your draft. Remember that no piece of writing is ever really finished. You may have some fresh ideas; add them to your draft. Look at Sebastian's and Cherry's essays. Borrow words and structures if you want.

EXCHANGE DRAFTS WITH YOUR READER

When you feel that your new draft is finished, give it to your reader. Your reader will give you his or her draft. You should read each other's drafts and write on them. Write comments like:

> This is very clear.

I don't understand this.
Interesting!

You may want to know more information. Write questions, such as:

Why do you like to do this?
Do you ever forget to do it?

Think about your routine. Is your reader's routine similar or different?

REWRITE YOUR DRAFT

Look at your essay and your reader's comments carefully. Rewrite your essay one more time. Your teacher may want to read the drafts and the final essay. Save this final essay and your drafts in your notebook.

Winding Down

Write a few lines in your learning log. Your teacher is your reader. For this unit, write to him or her about these questions:

Did you like writing about a routine?
Do you like to talk to your partner before you write?
Does he or she understand you when you speak?
Do you understand him or her?

Write about these questions or other things that you want your teacher to know. Give your paper to your teacher. He or she will read it, write some comments, and then return it to you to keep in your log.

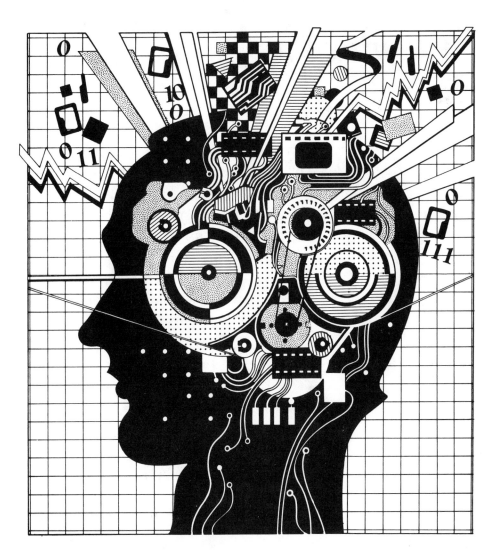

UNIT 4

SPECIAL OCCASIONS

Rhetorical Focus: Narration

Organizational Focus: Chronological Order

Grammatical Focus: Simple Present Tense Review

Warming Up

YOUR JOURNAL

Write in your journal for five minutes. Write about a special occasion—a holiday or celebration. Answer questions such as these:

What special occasions do you celebrate?
What does "special" mean?
What is special about the celebration?

Write words. Write sentences. Don't worry about correct grammar. Write whatever comes to mind. If you can't think of anything, write "I don't know what to write about a special occasion." Write it again until something comes to mind.

PLAYING WITH WORDS

1. Write a very *positive* sentence.
    Example: I learn more about writing every day.
2. Write a very *negative* sentence.
    Example: I will never learn to write well.

Share your sentences with your classmates.

GETTING READY TO READ

The essays in this unit are by Lien and Hassen. You already know Hassen from Unit 1. You know Lien from Units 1 and 2. They are writing about occasions that are special for them. You are the reader. What do you want to know?

1. Write questions that you want them to answer.
    Example: What is the special occasion?
2. Write words that you expect them to use in their essays.
    Example: holiday
                     celebrate

Share your questions and words with your classmates.

Reading 4A

Please read about Lien's special occasion:

CHINESE NEW YEAR

Chinese New Year is the most important holiday for Chinese people. We begin to prepare for the day a week before, and we continue to celebrate a week after. Food is a very important part of the holiday. We like to show off our good fortune in the way we prepare our food.

SUN.	MON.	TUE.	WED.	THUR.	FRI.	SAT.
		1	2	3	4	5
6	7 PREPARE	FOOD			11	12
⑬	14 CELEBRATE				18	19
20	21	22	23	24	25	26
27	28	29	30			

Every Chinese family serves different kinds of food for dinner on New Year's Eve. There are Chinese cakes on the table. In the Chinese culture, cakes are a symbol of prosperity. There are also dishes of chicken, pork, vegetables, and seafood. Fish is especially important. It is a symbol of excess, or surplus. Every Chinese family hopes to have more than enough food and clothes for the year ahead. People usually start their dinner late. This way, they can send off the old year and bring in the new year.

Families don't go to bed until two or three o'clock in the morning. Children are too excited to fall asleep anyway. In the morning, there will be many guests at the house. Friends and relatives always drop by on New Year's Day to bring red envelopes to the children. In the envelopes, there is money. On New Year's Day, children also light firecrackers, and everyone watches the parades on the streets.

I love Chinese New Year. It is full of excitement and joy. It is a time for families to give thanks for the old year. It is a time to wish for peace and prosperity in the year ahead.

RAMADAN ⟶ AID ELKEBIR

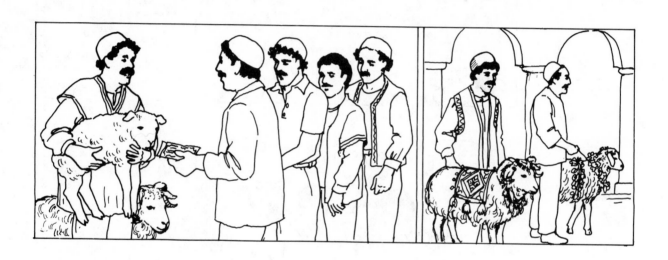

Reading 4B

Please read about a special holiday in Hassen's country:

AID ELKEBIR

Aid Elkebir is the name of a religious holiday for Moslems. It is my favorite holiday. It comes seventy-three days after the end of Ramadan every year. In Islam, Ramadan is the month of fasting. On Aid, we remember Abraham and his son, Isaac. Many centuries ago, Abraham was ready to kill his son as a gift to God. At the last moment, God sent a sheep. Abraham killed the sheep in Isaac's place. We remember this day by killing a sheep.

A month or two before Aid, families start buying their sheep. It is a good time for farmers; they sell many sheep. It is a difficult time for poor families who do not have the price of a sheep. About a week before Aid, families start showing off their sheep. They decorate their sheep. They walk their sheep in the street. People say, "Oh, my sheep is so fat" or "My sheep has such big, curly horns."

The night before Aid, nobody sleeps. The lights are on until morning. The streets are crowded. People buy balloons, toys, new clothes, and special candy for their children. Early in the morning, men and old people go to the mosque to pray. After prayers, people shake hands and wish each other a good year. On the way home, the head of the family buys special bread. This bread is in the shape of a wheel.

At home, the wives are busy. They cook and get everything ready. After the husband arrives home, he gently puts the sheep on the ground and says, "By God's name and God is the greatest." Then he kills the sheep. Afterwards, the husband goes from house to house in the neighborhood. He wishes everyone a good Aid. Later, the family gathers to eat "couscous," a special dish of cooked wheat with vegetables and lamb on top.

Aid is a time to enjoy the family, friends, and neighbors. It is a time to feel close to others. I love this holiday for its good food and warm spirit.

Exercises on the Readings

EXERCISE A: COMPREHENSION

Please circle the letters below to show the correct answers. The information comes from Lien's and Hassen's essays in this unit. If you don't know an answer, go back to their essays.

1. People begin to prepare for Chinese New Year
   a. two weeks before.
   b. one week before.
   c. the evening before.

2. In the way they prepare their food, Chinese families show off
   a. their good fortune.
   b. their excitement.
   c. their appetites.

3. Chinese cakes symbolize
   a. excess.
   b. happiness.
   c. prosperity.

4. Fish symbolizes
   a. excess.
   b. happiness.
   c. excitement.

5. On New Year's Day, children receive
   a. new clothes.
   b. money.
   c. special candy.

6. Islam is
   a. a religion.
   b. a holiday.
   c. a person.

7. "Aid Elkebir" and "Ramadan" are the names of two
   a. holy men.
   b. Tunisian towns.
   c. Islamic holidays.

8. On Aid, Moslems kill sheep in order to remember
   a. the history of their country.
   b. Abraham and Isaac.
   c. their grandparents.

9. The night before Aid, everyone
   a. buys a sheep.
   b. goes to bed early.
   c. stays up all night.

10. Hassen likes Aid for
    a. its warm spirit.
    b. its history.
    c. its color.

EXERCISE B: AGREEMENT

Please complete each sentence with a noun (singular or plural) from
the list below. The information comes from Lien's and Hassen's essays in this unit. The verbs and possessive adjectives will help you
choose the correct noun form.

wife	child	family	husband	dish
wives	children	families	husbands	dishes

1. On Chinese New Year's Day, each _____ receives a red envelope with money inside.

2. On New Year's, Chinese _____ show off their
   good fortune in the way they prepare their food.

3. On the table of every Chinese family, there are _____
   of chicken, pork, vegetables, and seafood.

4. By serving fish, every Chinese _____ wishes for
   an excess of food and clothes in the year ahead.

5. On Aid, the _____ are busy at home while their
   husbands go to the mosque to pray.

6. On their way home from the mosque, the _____
   stop at the bakery to buy special bread.

7. On Aid, _____ play with their new toys and eat
   their special candy.

8. The husband kills the sheep, and the _____ prepares the meat.

9. The wife cooks the holiday meal while the _____ visits each house in the neighborhood.

10. Couscous is the traditional _____ for dinner on Aid.

EXERCISE C: WORDWORK

Please complete each sentence with a word from the list below. The sentences help to define the meanings of the words.

religious	mosque	century	fortune	excess
prosperity	guest	excitement	fasting	holiday

1. Our _____ is our good luck. It can also be our wealth. Everyone who has good luck and wealth is truly fortunate!

2. When we earn money and prosper, we enjoy _____ .

3. When we have more than enough, we have an _____ .

4. _____ is the noun form of the word "excited."

5. A visitor to your house is a _____ .

6. A "holy day" that we celebrate becomes a _____ .

7. The adjective form of the word "religion" is _____ .

8. A time when people do not eat at all or eat very little is a time of _____ .

9. A hundred years is a _____ .

10. Christians attend religious services in a church, Jews go to a synagogue, Buddhists go to a temple, and Moslems go to a _____ .

Parallel Writing

Now that you have read Lien's and Hassen's essays, you are probably ready to write about a special occasion in your own culture. Remember that your essay will be parallel to Lien's and Hassen's, but it will probably be shorter and simpler than theirs. Follow these instructions.

TALK WITH A PARTNER

1. Choose a partner (the same partner or a different one). Tell your partner about a special occasion—a holiday or celebration. Include information such as:

☐ whether it is a holiday or a family celebration
☐ whether it happens every year
☐ how long the celebration lasts

Your partner will take notes. After you finish talking, ask your partner to read the notes back to you. Did he or she understand everything correctly? If not, tell him or her the correct information.

2. Now it's your partner's turn. Listen to your partner talk about a special occasion. Take notes. Then read your notes back to your partner. Did you understand everything? If not, your partner will tell you the correct information.

Now you know about a different holiday or celebration. Is it similar to the one you talked about?

MAKE SOME DECISIONS

Before you write your essay, you need to make these decisions:

Who is your reader? (Choose a different classmate each time.)

What does your reader want to know about your special occasion? What questions do you think he or she wants you to answer? (Think about what you and your partner talked about and write down some questions.)

WRITE A DRAFT

Write a draft of an essay about a holiday or celebration. Remember that a draft is not the final essay. Answer the questions that you wrote, but don't write the questions. Write your sentences in paragraph form. As you write, you may get more ideas. Include them in your draft.

READ ALOUD TO YOUR PARTNER

1. Read your draft aloud to your partner (not your reader). Your partner should listen carefully and think about these questions:

> Is the information clear?
> Is something not clear?
> What else do I want to know?

Your partner will probably make comments while you read. If your partner says that an idea is not clear, write it in a different way. Your partner may make other comments after you finish reading. Remember that the purpose of these comments is to help you write better, not to say what is right and what is wrong.

2. Ask your partner to read your draft to you. Listen to it as a stranger might listen to it. Are the ideas clear? Is it interesting? Is there anything else that you want to say?

3. Now change roles with your partner. Listen to your partner's draft. Talk about it together. Then read the draft aloud to your partner.

WRITE A SECOND DRAFT

Rework your draft. Remember that no piece of writing is ever really finished. You may get some new ideas as you write; add them to your draft. Look at Lien's and Hassen's essays. You may get some ideas that you can add to your draft.

EXCHANGE DRAFTS WITH YOUR READER

When you feel that your new draft is finished, give it to your reader.

Your reader will give you his or her draft. You should read each other's drafts and write on them. Write comments like:

> This is very clear.
> I don't understand this.
> This is interesting.

You may want to know more information. If so, write questions such as, Why do people like to do this?

REWRITE YOUR DRAFT

Look at your essay and your reader's comments carefully. Rewrite your essay one more time. Your teacher may want to read the drafts and the final essay. Save this final essay and your drafts in your notebook.

Winding Down

Write a few lines in your learning log. Write to your teacher. Write to him or her about these questions:

> Did you like writing about a special occasion?
> Was it easier or more difficult than the other essays?
> Do you like writing in your learning log?
> Does it help your writing?

Write about these questions or other things that you want your teacher to know. Give your paper to your teacher to read. He or she will write some comments and then return it to you to keep in your log.

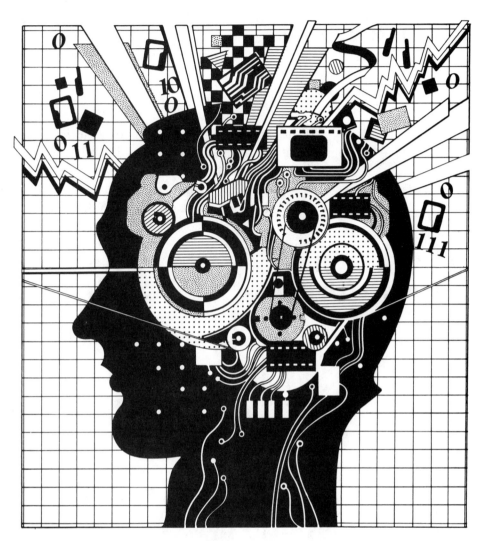

UNIT 5

FAVORITE PLACES

Rhetorical Focus: Description

Organizational Focus: Spatial Order

Grammatical Focus: Present Continuous Tense Review

Warming Up

YOUR JOURNAL

Write in your journal for five minutes. Write about your favorite place in the world. Where is it? What does "favorite" mean? What makes this place special?

Write words, phrases, or sentences. Write anything that comes to mind. If you can't think of anything, write "I don't know what to write about my favorite place." Write it again until something comes to mind.

PLAYING WITH WORDS

1. Write a "d" sentence, in which all the important words start with *d*.

    Example: The dark dancer dances during dinner.
2. Write a "c" sentence.

    Example: The cute couple can't call the company.
3. Write a sentence for another letter that you choose.

Share your sensational sentences with some super students!

GETTING READY TO READ

The essays in this unit are by Hassen and Lien. They are writing about their favorite places. You are the reader. What do you want to know?

1. Write questions that you want them to answer.

    Example: What is your favorite place?
2. Write words that you expect them to use in their essays.

    Example: go
                       like

Share your words and questions with your classmates.

Reading 5A

Please read about Lien's favorite place:

ON A MOUNTAINTOP

My favorite place is a little Buddhist temple near my childhood home. It is on top of a mountain. There are no roads to the temple. There are stairs up the mountain. It takes about an hour to climb thousands of stairs to the top. I can close my eyes and see the temple now.

    The morning air is fresh and cool. I am climbing the stairs to the top. It is early. There are still drops of water on the leaves of the trees from the night rain. It is quiet and still. Birds are singing. I reach the top, and I look down far below. The cars and bicycles are very tiny. There is not much traffic on the streets. In front of the temple, there is a courtyard. In the courtyard, monks are studying and praying. The temple is

red and gold, with a touch of green. Inside the temple, there are three Buddhas. One takes care of all the evil in the world. One takes care of nature. I am there to see the third Buddha. The third one takes care of people's fate. I confess and say my prayers. I turn and leave.

In the courtyard, the monks are still praying. On my way down the mountain, the birds are still singing. The leaves are dry now. Below, there is more traffic. I feel quiet and peaceful as I go down the mountain.

Reading 5B

Please read about Hassen's favorite place:

MY ISLAND

Ramadia is a little island near my childhood home. I spent the happiest days of my childhood there. Almost every summer morning, I took my little boat and sailed to Ramadia. I sometimes dream abut Ramadia. In my dreams, I am there.

The island is small and round. It rises high above the sea. From a distance, it looks like a stage. I can see myself now. I am sitting on a rocky cliff. The sun is rising in the distance. The sea birds are waking up and flying over the island. Now and then, I hear a sea gull. It is diving for fish. In front of me, small boats are sailing by. The fishermen are going out to sea for the day. The air is quiet, and I can hear them talking and singing. Down below me, the water is clear. Small crabs and fish are swimming around and looking for food. At one end of the island, there is a tall palm tree. According to my grandfather, the tree is there to help fishermen find land during bad

weather. To the west and across the sea, there are fields. Sheep and camels are grazing there. At sunset, I can hear the voices of the shepherds. They are driving their animals home. After sunset, the island is still and quiet. Then the wind starts blowing from the north and stirs the water.

Ramadia is a place of peace and quiet during the day. At night, it is a frightening place. The roaring waves frighten me. The roaring waves are mad lions that are coming to jump on me. I love the peacefulness and the madness of the island.

Exercises on the Readings

EXERCISE A: COMPREHENSION

Please circle the letters below to show the correct answers. The information comes from Lien's and Hassen's essays in this unit. If you don't know an answer, go back to their essays.

1. Lien's favorite place is
    a. a mountain.
    b. her childhood home.
    c. a Buddhist temple.

2. In order to get to her favorite place, Lien has to
    a. drive up a steep road.
    b. climb thousands of stairs.
    c. take a train.

3. Lien likes to go there
    a. in the morning.
    b. in the afternoon.
    c. in the evening.

4. In front of the temple, there is
    a. a statue of Buddha.
    b. a tall tree.
    c. a courtyard.

5. Lien prays to the Buddha who takes care of
    a. people's fate.
    b. all the evil in the world.
    c. nature.

6. Hassen's favorite place is
    a. a field.
    b. an island.
    c. a rocky cliff.

7. Hassen gets to his favorite place
    a. on foot.
    b. by boat.
    c. by swimming across a little river.

8. From his favorite place, Hassen hears the voices of
   a. mermaids.
   b. only shepherds.
   c. shepherds and fishermen.

9. A tall palm tree is there
   a. to provide shade for animals.
   b. to make the island more beautiful.
   c. to help fishermen find land.

10. At night, Ramadia is
    a. wild.
    b. quiet.
    c. peaceful.

EXERCISE B: PRESENT CONTINUOUS TENSE

Please write complete sentences for each group of words below. Use
She/he/it is . . . + *-ing* or *They are* . . . + *-ing*. The time is NOW.

> Example: Lien . . . (climb) the stairs to the temple.
> *She is climbing the stairs to the temple.*

1. Birds . . . . (sing)

   _____

2. Monks . . . . (study)

   _____

3. Monks . . . . (pray)

   _____

4. The sun . . . . (shine)

   _____

5. Hassen . . . (sail) his little boat to Ramadia.

   _____

6. Hassen . . . (sit) on a rocky cliff.

   _____

7. A sea gull . . . (dive) for fish.

   _____

8. The fishermen . . . (go) out to sea.

   _____

9. Small crabs and fish . . . (swim) around in the clear water.

_____

10. Sheep and camels . . . (graze) in the fields to the west.

_____

EXERCISE C: SPATIAL ORDER

Please put the sentences below into proper order. The order is according to space.

1. The courtyard is in front of the temple.
2. From the bottom of the mountain, there are stairs.
3. Across the courtyard, there is a small door.
4. The stairs lead to the courtyard.

The correct order is _____ , _____ , _____ , and _____ .

1. Inside the temple, there are three Buddhas.
2. In the courtyard, monks are praying.
3. As you approach the temple, you see a courtyard.
4. People are praying in front of the Buddhas.

The correct order is _____ , _____ , _____ , and _____ .

1. The Buddha to the right takes care of people's fate.
2. The Buddha in the middle takes care of nature.
3. The Buddha to the left takes care of the evil in the world.
4. Inside the temple, there are three statues of Buddha.

The correct order is _____ , _____ , _____ , and _____ .

1. It heads toward the island.
2. The little boat leaves shore.
3. In front of it, the island gets larger.
4. Behind it, the houses on the shore get smaller.

The correct order is _____ , _____ , _____ , and _____ .

1. Hassen is sitting on a rocky cliff.
2. Far below him, fish are swimming in the clear water.
3. On the rocks next to him, sea birds are singing.
4. Across the sea, sheep are grazing in the fields.

The correct order is _____ , _____ , _____ , and _____ .

Parallel Writing

Now that you have read about Lien's and Hassen's favorite places, you are probably ready to write about your own. Remember that your essay will be parallel, but not exactly the same as theirs. It may be shorter and simpler. Follow these instructions.

TALK WITH A PARTNER

1. Choose a partner (the same partner or a new one). Tell your partner about your favorite place. Imagine that you are there now. Describe it, using many details. Help your partner to see it in his or her mind. Explain why it is special.

Your partner will take notes. After you finish talking, ask your partner to read the notes back to you. Listen carefully. Did he or she understand everything? If not, tell your partner the correct information.

2. Now it's your partner's turn. Listen to your partner describe his or her favorite place. Take notes. Then read your notes back to your partner. Did you understand everything? If not, your partner will help you write the correct information.

MAKE SOME DECISIONS

Before you write your essay, you need to make these decisions:

Who is your reader? (Choose a classmate.)

What does your reader want to know about your favorite place? What questions do you think he or she wants you to answer? (Think about what you and your partner talked about and write down some questions.)

WRITE A DRAFT

Write a draft of an essay about your favorite place. Remember, a draft is not the final essay. Answer the questions that you wrote, but don't write the questions. Write your sentences in paragraph form. As you write, you may think of more details. Include them in your draft.

READ ALOUD TO YOUR PARTNER

1. Read your draft aloud to your partner (not your reader). Your partner should listen carefully and think about these questions:

> Is the description clear?
> Is any part of it not clear?
> Can I see the place in my mind?
> What else do I want to know?

Your partner may make comments while you read or after you finish reading. Remember that the purpose of these comments is to help you write better, not to say what is right and what is wrong. If your partner says that something is not clear, try writing it in a different way.

2. Ask your partner to read your draft to you. Listen to it as a stranger might listen to it. Can you picture the place? Do the details help you see it?

3. Now change roles with your partner. Listen to your partner's draft. Talk about it together. Then read the draft aloud to your partner.

WRITE A SECOND DRAFT

Rework your draft. Remember that all writers need to rework their writing. Look at Hassen's and Lien's essays. They may give you some new ideas that you can include in your draft.

EXCHANGE DRAFTS WITH YOUR READER

When you feel that your new draft is finished, give it to your reader. Your reader will give you his or her draft. You should read each other's drafts and write on them. Write comments like:

> This is a good detail.
> I don't understand this.
> Can you write more about this?

Think about your favorite place. How is your reader's favorite place similar? How is it different?

REWRITE YOUR DRAFT

Look at your essay and your reader's comments carefully. Rewrite your essay one more time. Your teacher may want to read the drafts and the final essay. Save this final essay and your drafts in your notebook.

Winding Down

Write a few lines in your learning log. Your teacher is your reader. For this unit, write about your writing. What part of the writing process helps you the most:

☐ talking to your partner?
☐ thinking about your reader's questions?
☐ reading the essays in the book?

Write about these questions or other things that you want your teacher to know. Give your paper to your teacher. He or she will read it, write some comments, and then return it to you to keep in your log.

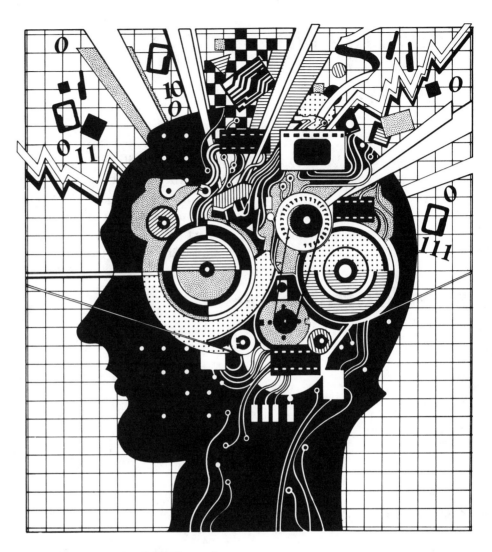

UNIT 6

DAILY ACTIVITIES

Rhetorical Focus: Narration

Organizational Focus: Chronological Order

Grammatical Focus: Complex/Compound Sentence Review

Warming Up

YOUR JOURNAL

Write in your journal for five minutes. Write about people whom you know well and their daily activities. Do they do the same thing every day? How do they feel about what they're doing?

Write words, phrases, and sentences. Write whatever comes to mind. Don't worry about correct grammar. If you can't think of anything, write "I don't know what to write about daily activities." Write it again until something comes to mind.

PLAYING WITH WORDS

1. Write a *loving* sentence.

     Example: She is the light of my life!
2. Write a *hateful* sentence.

     Example: He is a horrible person.

Share your sentences with your classmates. Be careful with hateful sentences. They are like bombs that might explode.

GETTING READY TO READ

The essays in this unit are by Sebastian and Cherry. They are writing about the daily activities of someone they know very well. You are the reader. What do you want to know about their topic?

1. Write questions that you want them to answer.

     Example: Whom are you writing about?
2. Write words that you expect them to use in their essays.

     Example: morning
                every (afternoon, evening, day, etc.)

Share your questions and words with your classmates.

Reading 6A

Please read about Sebastian's mother's daily activities:

MY MOTHER'S WORK

My mother's job is interesting, but it is very demanding. She is the Consul of Honduras in New Orleans. She works hard, and she has many things to do every day.

    She is in her office at eight o'clock every morning, Monday through Friday. She sometimes has to go in on the weekends, too. She starts each day with a brief meeting with her staff. At these meetings, she gives them information, answers questions, solves problems, and tells them about any special activities for

that day. Her office issues passports and visas, promotes trade
with Honduras, and handles important documents for citizens
of Honduras. There are also some unpleasant duties. If there
are illegal Hondurans in New Orleans, her office must process
the papers to deport them.

The consulate closes at three o'clock in the afternoon, but
my mother never leaves the office then. She always stays to
handle special problems. There is always someone who needs a
visa right away for an emergency trip to Honduras. Sometimes,
she has to replace a lost passport for someone who is leaving
for Honduras that same day.

My mother's day is not over even after she leaves the office.

She is on call twenty-four hours a day. Last Sunday, someone called her at 1:30 in the morning to request some emergency documents. A Honduran national had died, and the relatives needed documents to take the body to Honduras for burial. Also, she attends many meetings in the evenings. For example, she meets with the Chamber of Commerce if they want to talk about trade with Latin America.

My mother loves her work. It is tiring work, but she feels good about helping so many people. She also loves New Orleans. There are so many Hondurans in New Orleans that she feels right at home.

Reading 6B

Please read about Cherry's grandmother's daily activities:

MEEM AND HER DAY

I remember the year 1967 very well. That was the year that my older sister started kindergarten, and I stayed home all day with my grandmother. We called her "Meem." My mother, sister, and I lived with her and my grandfather in the small town of Marksville, Louisiana. I remember Meem's days as well as my own.

     She always woke up early to fix my grandfather's breakfast. She always fixed the same thing for him: a fried egg on toast with orange juice and coffee. For herself, she prepared a milkshake. I don't know what she put in her milkshake, but it always seemed to get her going with a smile.

After my grandfather and mother left for work and my sister left for school, Meem came to wake me up. The noise of the blender from the kitchen usually woke me up first. When Meem got to my room, I was often up and in front of the TV. My favorite early-morning cartoon was "Polycarp and His Pals," the Cajun version of Captain Kangaroo. After the cartoon was over, I went to the kitchen with Meem to wait for Lucille, the maid.

'Cille arrived about nine every morning. Meem then went down her list of things for 'Cille to do. 'Cille listened, nodded her head, took notes, and then ignored the list completely. 'Cille had her own way of doing things. She ran the house, and they both knew it. Meem always went through her little routine anyway.

By mid-morning, it was time to wait for Lydee. Lydee was the vegetable lady. She had the largest garden in town, and every morning she drove her ancient truck full of vegetables around to all the houses. Lydee was a large woman, and she spoke in a strong Cajun accent. She spoke very fast, half-French and half-English. Meem never quite knew what she was buying. As a result, we ate some interesting vegetables.

After lunch, Meem did her afternoon "phone work." In Marksville, as in any small town, there was an "old-girl" system at work. These were women who knew all of the town's business and practically ran the town. Meem had the ability to know what was going to happen before it happened, but her phone work helped.

After her phone work, she always took the dictionary from the shelf to teach me new words. She always picked words that were difficult to pronounce and were of no use to a four-year-old. I learned them anyway. Meem made it fun. By the time I started kindergarten the next year, I had a bigger vocabulary than any kid in town.

After supper, Meem always read a bedtime story to me and my sister. She took us on long journeys far beyond Marksville, but she always got us back in time for bed. Even as a little kid, I knew that every day with Meem was extraordinary.

Exercises on the Readings

EXERCISE A: COMPREHENSION

Please circle the letters below to show the correct answers. The information comes from Sebastian's and Cherry's essays in this unit. If you don't know an answer, go back to their essays.

1. Sebastian's mother is
   a. the Honduran Consul.
   b. a secretary.
   c. the Mayor of New Orleans.

2. She starts work at
   a. 1:30 A.M.
   b. 7:00 A.M.
   c. 8:00 A.M.

3. Her office
   a. issues passports and visas.
   b. sends bodies to Honduras for burial.
   c. meets with the Chamber of Commerce.

4. In the evenings, she often
   a. relaxes and watches television.
   b. attends meetings.
   c. visits Honduran nationals.

5. Sebastian thinks that his mother's job is
   a. very relaxing.
   b. very demanding.
   c. very boring.

6. "Meem" is the nickname of Cherry's
   a. grandfather.
   b. grandmother.
   c. sister.

7. When Cherry was small, she lived with
   a. her grandmother, grandfather, mother, and sister.
   b. her grandmother, father, mother, and sister.
   c. Lucille, Lydee, her grandmother, and sister.

8. 'Cille was their
   a. grandfather's sister.
   b. vegetable lady.
   c. maid.

9. Lydee delivered vegetables in her
   a. old truck.
   b. new truck.
   c. old van.

10. After lunch, Meem
    a. bought vegetables.
    b. took a nap.
    c. talked on the telephone.

EXERCISE B: CONNECTIONS

Please complete the sentences below with words from the following list:

after	before	and
but	when	because

You will need to use some of these connecting words more than once.

1. At staff meetings, Sebastian's mother gives information _____ answers questions.

2. The Honduran Consulate closes at 3:00 P.M. every day, _____ Sebastian's mother never leaves the office then.

3. Her day is not over even _____ she leaves the office.

4. _____ she wants to promote trade with Honduras, she sometimes meets with business groups in the evening.

5. Her work is tiring, _____ she feels good about helping so many people.

6. Cherry stayed home with her grandmother _____ she was too young to go to school.

7. Cherry's grandmother always came in to wake her up
   _____ everyone else had left for work and
   school.

8. The noise of the blender usually woke Cherry up _____
   her grandmother came in.

9. She was usually watching her favorite cartoon _____
   her grandmother walked in.

10. Cherry's grandmother didn't understand Lydee very well
    _____ she spoke fast and used a lot of French
    words.

EXERCISE C: PREPOSITIONS

Please complete the sentences below with prepositions from the following list:

in	at	to	with
for	on	of	

You will need to use each preposition more than once.

Sebastian's mother is _____ her office _____ eight o'clock
every morning, Monday through Friday. She sometimes has _____
go _____ her office _____ the weekends, too. She starts each workday
_____ a brief staff meeting. _____ these meetings, she briefs her
staff. She and her staff have many duties. They issue passports and
visas, promote trade, and handle important documents _____
citizens _____ Honduras. She and her staff also have some
unpleasant duties. If there are illegal Hondurans _____ New
Orleans, her office must process the papers _____ deport them.

The consulate closes _____ three o'clock every afternoon, but
Mrs. Pastor never leaves the office _____ that time. She always stays
_____ handle special problems. There is always someone who needs
a visa immediately _____ an emergency trip _____ Honduras.
Sometimes, she has to replace a lost passport _____ someone who
is leaving _____ Honduras that same day.

Mrs. Pastor's day is not over even after she leaves the office. She is _____ call twenty-four hours a day. Last Sunday, for example, someone called her at 1:30 _____ the morning _____ request some emergency documents. A Honduran national had died, and the relatives needed documents _____ take the body _____ Honduras _____ burial. Her work never seems _____ end.

Parallel Writing

Now that you have read Sebastian's and Cherry's essays, you may have some good ideas for your own writing. Remember that your essay will be parallel, but not exactly the same as theirs. It may be shorter and simpler. Follow these instructions.

TALK WITH A PARTNER

1. Choose a partner (the same partner or a different one). Tell your partner about the daily activities of someone you know well. Tell who the person is. Describe the activities. They will help you describe the person.

Your partner will take notes. After you finish talking, ask your partner to read the notes back to you. Did he or she understand everything correctly? If not, tell him or her the correct information.

2. Now it's your partner's turn. Listen to your partner talk about someone else's daily activities. Take notes. Then read your notes back to your partner. Did you understand everything? If not, your partner will help you write the correct information.

MAKE SOME DECISIONS

Before you write your essay, you need to make these decisions:

Who is your reader? (Choose a classmate.)

What does your reader want to know about this person's activities? What questions do you think he or she wants you to answer? (Think about what you and your partner talked about and write down some questions.)

WRITE A DRAFT

Write a draft of an essay about someone's daily activities. Remember that a draft is not the final essay. Answer the questions that you wrote, but don't write the questions. Write your sentences in paragraph form. As you write, you may get more ideas. Include them in your draft.

READ ALOUD TO YOUR PARTNER

1. Read your draft aloud to your partner (not your reader). Your partner should listen carefully and think about these questions:

> Are the activities clear?
> Is something not clear?
> Does the order of activities make sense?
> What else do I want to know?

Your partner may make comments while you read or after you finish reading. Remember that the purpose of these comments is to help you write better, not to say what is right and what is wrong. If your partner says that something is not clear, try writing it in a different way.

2. Ask your partner to read your draft to you. Listen to it as a stranger might listen to it. How does it sound? Are the ideas clear? Is there anything else that you want to say?

3. Now change roles with your partner. Listen to your partner's draft. Talk about it together. Then read the draft aloud to your partner.

WRITE A SECOND DRAFT

Rework your draft. Remember that no piece of writing is ever really finished. Think about different ways to say something. Look at Sebastian's and Cherry's essays. You may get some ideas that you can add to your draft.

EXCHANGE DRAFTS WITH YOUR READER

When you feel that your new draft is finished, give it to your reader. Your reader will give you his or her draft. You should read each other's drafts and write on them. Write comments like:

> This is interesting.
> I don't understand this.
> Is something missing here?
> Can you tell me more about this?

Compare your reader's essay with yours. What is similar? What is different?

REWRITE YOUR DRAFT

Look at your essay and your reader's comments carefully, then rewrite your essay one more time. Your teacher may want to read this final version and the other drafts. Save both in your notebook.

Winding Down

Write a half-page in your learning log. Write to your teacher. Did you enjoy this unit's assignment? Did you learn anything new about writing? Can you compare writing in English with writing in your native language?

Write about these questions or other things that you want your teacher to know. Give your paper to your teacher to read. He or she will write some comments and then return it to you to keep in your log.

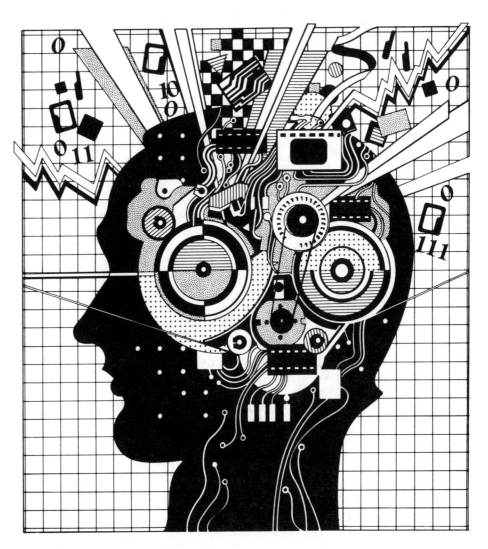

UNIT 7

CONTACTS

Rhetorical Focus: Narration

Organizational Focus: Shift of Conversational Subject

Grammatical Focus: Present Continuous Tense Review

Warming Up

YOUR JOURNAL

Write in your journal for five or ten minutes. "Talk" to someone you know well, someone you haven't seen for a long time. Imagine that the person is sitting across from you. What do you want to say to him or her?

Write words, phrases, and sentences. Write whatever comes to mind. Don't worry about correct grammar. If you can't think of anything, write "I don't know what to say to you." Keep writing it until something comes to mind.

PLAYING WITH WORDS

1. Write five ways to greet someone.

    Example:　Hi!

2. Write five names to call a loved one.

    Example:　Honey

Share your words with your classmates.

GETTING READY TO READ

The writing in this unit is by Lien and Cherry. Their writing is in the form of personal letters. They are writing to people they know well. This is their way to keep in touch with people far away. The letters are not written to you, but you can read them. What do you want Lien and Cherry to tell you?

1. Write questions that you want to ask them.

    Example:　To whom are you writing?

2. Write words that you expect them to use in their letters.

    Example:　Dear
    　　　　　　family

Share your questions and words with your classmates.

Reading 7A

Please read Lien's letter to her cousin, Chi:

October 2, 1988

Dear Chi,

I am listening to the radio, and it is playing your favorite song, "Morning Has Broken." That was eight years ago, remember? The song reminds me of you. I miss you very much. I am here alone in my room now. I am daydreaming about our times together.

It is October now, and in New Orleans it is still summer! The heat is still too much for me. In a few more weeks, it will get cooler. I feel restless when the summer heat hangs on for so long.

How are you? Are you still taking a lot of pictures? I can see you busy in your darkroom now. Chi, you should come here. New Orleans is a beautiful city for photographs. The people and

buildings make interesting subjects. Both tell interesting stories. There are the old men in the French Market who sell wa-
termelons and garlic. There is Ruthie, the Duck Lady, who
roller-skates through the French Quarter with her duck. There
are the jugglers and magicians who perform in Jackson
Square. You love to capture stories with your camera, don't
you? Come to New Orleans.

How are your sister and brother? How are your mother
and father? I hope that everyone is well. Tell them hello for me.
Tell them that I miss them, too.

Love,

Lien

Reading 7B

Please read Cherry's letter to her friend, Bonnie:

October 25, 1988

Dear Bonnie,

   I'm sitting in my room and looking through my old record albums. There's one here that reminds me of you, one by Jethro Tull. Do you remember? We played that record together every afternoon for over a year. I was so sure then that my life would be perfect in five or six years. Well, here I am five years later. I

have the same worries about money and school. I'm not married to a prince or living in a magic kingdom. I'm living in New Orleans, and I'm not married at all.

I went back to Alexandria several months ago. I stopped in front of your old house on Levin Street. It really looks different! It is a strange color that's not quite yellow and not quite orange. I'm glad that you're in Connecticut. You don't have to look at it. It makes me sad to think that someone else is living in your house.

I am still working my way through school. I'll graduate in a year or two, if I'm lucky. Of course, you know that I change my mind a lot. My major is now English, not sociology. After I get my degree, I might teach. I'm not sure. Teachers don't earn very much money. Maybe I'll know what I want to do when I grow up. Here I am; I'm twenty-three, and I don't know what I want to be. Oh, well!

I'm still working part-time at a local hospital. The job is so boring! Watching a potato bake in a microwave is more exciting. I'm working in the English Department at school, too. That job is a little more interesting, but not much.

Do you still go to the movies a lot? Since movie tickets are so expensive, I don't go much any more. Instead, I find friends who have cable TV and VCR's, and I watch movies at their houses. It's much cheaper that way. I still read as much as ever. I don't mind paying for a good book.

This letter is turning out to be too long. I'll say goodbye. Write soon with stories of life in Connecticut. Take care of yourself. Think of me when you listen to Jethro Tull.

Love,

Cherry

Exercises on the Readings

EXERCISE A: COMPREHENSION

Please circle the letters below to show the correct answers. The information comes from Lien's and Cherry's letters in this unit. If you don't know an answer, go back to their letters.

1. Lien is writing to
    a. her friend, Chi.
    b. her sister, Chi.
    c. her cousin, Chi.

2. While she is writing the letter, she is sitting
    a. in the library at school.
    b. in her room at home.
    c. in a darkroom in a photography studio.

3. From Lien's letter, we know that Chi is interested in
    a. photography.
    b. old men.
    c. juggling and magic.

4. Lien tries to interest Chi in coming to visit
    a. by telling her about the weather in New Orleans.
    b. by inviting her.
    c. by giving examples of interesting people to photograph.

5. From Lien's letter, we know that Chi
    a. is an only child.
    b. has a brother and a sister.
    c. is an orphan.

6. Cherry is writing a letter to
    a. her friend, Bonnie.
    b. her cousin, Bonnie.
    c. her sister, Bonnie.

7. While she is writing the letter, she is sitting
    a. in the library at school.
    b. in a room at the hospital where she works.
    c. in her room at home.

8. From Cherry's letter, we know that Bonnie
   a. lives in Connecticut.
   b. lives in Alexandria, Louisiana.
   c. lives in New Orleans.

9. Cherry tells Bonnie that she is majoring in
   a. English.
   b. sociology.
   c. medical technology.

10. We know that Cherry
    a. eats potatoes.
    b. likes to read.
    c. owns a VCR.

EXERCISE B: PRESENT CONTINUOUS TENSE

Please answer the questions below with the correct information about Lien and Cherry.

> Example: Is Lien listening to records on her stereo?
> *No, she is listening to the radio.*

1. Is the radio station playing Lien's favorite song?

   _____

2. Is Lien writing a letter to Chi at the kitchen table?

   _____

3. Is Lien daydreaming about her boyfriend?

   _____

4. Is Lien inviting Chi to visit **New York?**

   _____

5. Is Cherry listening **to the radio** in her room?

   _____

6. Is Cherry still worrying about her hair?

   _____

7. Is Cherry living in Alexandria?

   _____

8. Is Cherry's friend, Bonnie, living in New Orleans?

   _____

9. Is Cherry majoring in sociology?

_____

10. Is Cherry working part-time at a Chinese restaurant?

_____

EXERCISE C: PUNCTUATION

A young man named Pete is writing a letter to his cousin, George. He has forgotten all the commas, periods, and question marks. Please add them for him.

October 12, 1988

Dear George

    It is a nice fall day and I am sitting in the park near my house It is early afternoon and I am thinking of you There are a few people in the park Some of them are strolling Others are sitting on park benches and reading Several people are riding their bicycles

    I am fine I like Chicago I already have a job in a hardware store The pay is not very good but I meet many interesting people They talk to me and ask a lot of questions They usually want to know how to repair something Today I have the afternoon off That's why I have time to write to you

    I hope that you are well and happy How is your school work Are you learning a lot of English Can you read this letter Are your classmates interesting Do you have a girlfriend How are your parents Please say hello to them for me Write soon I'll look forward to your letter

Your cousin

Pete

Parallel Writing

Now that you have read Lien's and Cherry's letters, you are ready to write your own. Choose an actual person to write to (someone who can read English). When you finish the letter, mail it to him or her. Follow these instructions.

TALK WITH A PARTNER

1. Choose a partner. Tell your partner the name of the person you are going to write to. Explain who this person is and why you want to write to him or her. Then tell your partner what you want to say in your letter.

Your partner will take notes. After you finish talking, ask your partner to read the notes back to you. Did your partner understand everything?

2. Now it is your partner's turn. Listen and take notes. Then read your notes back to your partner. Make sure you have the correct information.

MAKE SOME DECISIONS

This time, your decisions are a little different:

To whom are you going to write? (Remember, you should actually mail the letter.)

What does your reader want to know about you? (Write down some questions that come to mind.)

WRITE A DRAFT

Write a draft of your letter. Answer the questions that you wrote, but don't write the questions. Write your sentences in letter form. As you write, you may get new ideas. Include them in your letter.

READ ALOUD TO YOUR PARTNER

1. Read your draft aloud to your partner. Your partner should listen carefully and think about these questions:

> Is everything clear?
> Is something not clear?
> Is something missing?

Your partner may make comments while you read or after you finish reading. As you read, you may hear things that you want to change. Make as many changes as you want.

2. Ask your partner to read your draft to you. Imagine that you are the person who receives the letter. How does it sound? Is there anything else that you want to say?

3. Now change roles with your partner. Listen to your partner's letter and make suggestions. Then read the letter aloud to your partner.

WRITE A SECOND DRAFT

Rework your letter. Think about different ways to say the same idea. Look at Lien's and Cherry's letters. You may get some ideas that you can add to your letter.

EXCHANGE DRAFTS WITH YOUR PARTNER

This time, exchange drafts with your partner instead of your reader. Write comments and suggestions on each other's drafts. Write comments like:

> This is interesting.
> I don't understand this.
> Is something missing here?

Compare your partner's letter with yours. Is it similar? What is different?

REWRITE YOUR DRAFT

Look at your letter again and your partner's comments. Then write a final version of the letter. Your teacher may want to read this final version and the drafts. Save the drafts in your notebook and mail your letter. (See the following example of how to address an envelope.) When you receive an answer to your letter, you may want to share it with the class.

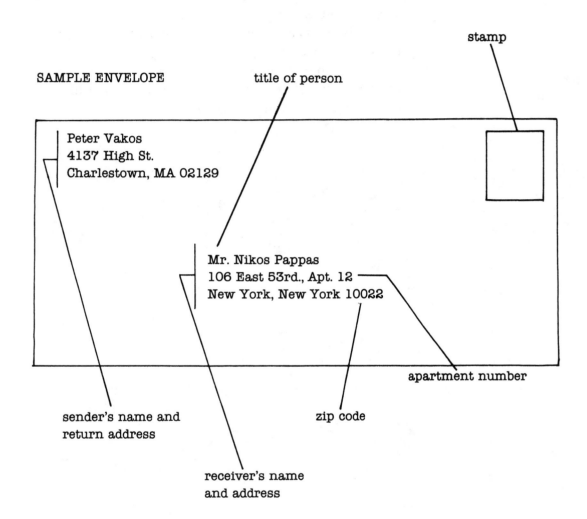

SAMPLE ENVELOPE

stamp

title of person

Peter Vakos
4137 High St.
Charlestown, MA 02129

Mr. Nikos Pappas
106 East 53rd., Apt. 12
New York, New York 10022

apartment number

sender's name and
return address

zip code

receiver's name
and address

Winding Down

Write at least a half-page in your learning log. Write to your teacher. Write about writing a letter. How is it different from writing an essay? Is it easier or harder? Do you like to write letters in your native language?

Write about these questions or other things that you want your teacher to know. Your teacher will read your writing, add some comments, and then return it to you to keep in your log.

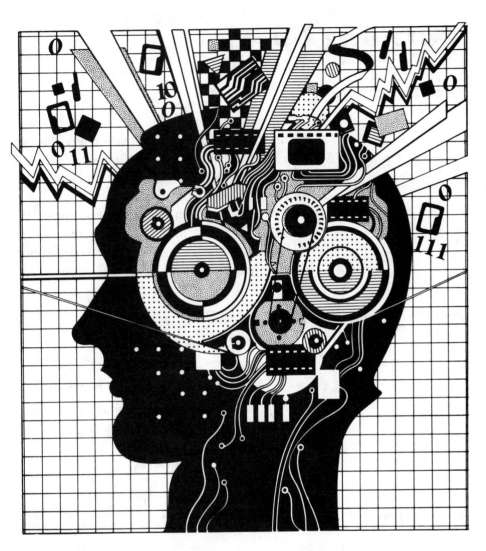

UNIT 8
FAMILIAR PLACES

Rhetorical Focus: Description

Organizational Focus: Spatial Order

Grammatical Focus: Simple Present
and Simple Past Tense Review

111

Warming Up

YOUR JOURNAL

Write in your journal for five or ten minutes. Write about a place that is very familiar to you, such as your room, your childhood home, or the playground at your old school. What did it look like? What memories does it bring back?

Write words, phrases, and sentences. Write whatever comes to mind. Don't worry about correct grammar. If you can't think of anything, write "I don't know what to write about a familiar place." Keep writing it until something comes to mind.

PLAYING WITH WORDS

1. Write three ways to say "Enter!"

    Example: The door is open!

2. Write three ways to ask someone to leave.

    Example: Go away! (This is very strong.)

Share your words with your classmates.

GETTING READY TO READ

The essays in this unit are by Sebastian and Cherry. They are writing about places that are familiar to them. You are the reader. What questions do you have for them?

1. Write questions that you want them to answer about their familiar places.

    Example: What place are you writing about?

2. Write words that you expect them to use in their essays.
    Example: small
              room

Share your questions and words with your classmates.

Reading 8A

Please read Sebastian's essay about a familiar place:

MY OLD ROOM

I remember many places from my childhood, but there is one place I remember best. It is my room in my old house in Honduras. My parents, my brother, and I lived in that house in Tegucigalpa, the capital of Honduras, for ten years. My room was on the second floor.

I remember many details about that room. It was rectangular in shape, and the ceiling was very high. The walls were white. The floors were wooden. I remember it as a large room, but it was probably of normal size. On the outside wall, there was a large window. Through the window, we were able to see the lights of the city at night. On either side of the window, there was a bed, one for my twin brother and one for me. It was actually "our" room; we shared it. Under the window, there was a writing desk with two chairs. This is where we did our

Sebastians Room

homework. On the adjacent wall, there were two doors. One opened into a closet, and the other led to a bathroom. On the wall opposite the window, there was a chest of drawers with several pictures above it. One picture was of my mother and father. Another was of Modesto Rodas Alvarado, a great Honduran political leader. On that wall, there were also awards that my brother and I had earned for being good students in elementary school.

Many beautiful memories go with that room. One time, the President of Honduras came to visit my father. I was in my room doing my homework, and my father brought him into my room to meet me. I will never forget that! I also remember the times when I woke up hungry in the middle of the night. I would get up and head out of my room to go to the kitchen for a snack. Often, I would run into my father coming out of my parents' room across the hall. He was on his way to the refrigerator, too. Oh, I wonder if I will ever see that room again.

Reading 8B

Please read about one of Cherry's familiar places:

FAMILIAR BUT NOT FAVORITE

These days, my most familiar place is the hospital office where I work. I work in the Office of Medical Records. I spend so much time there. I am thinking of putting a bed in one corner and listing it as my home address.

To reach Medical Records, you enter through the emergency room, take a left at the first hall and a right at the second. The halls here are like hospital halls everywhere. They are shiny, wide, and quiet. Since I work in the evening, the halls are especially quiet. The walls are covered with pictures. Some

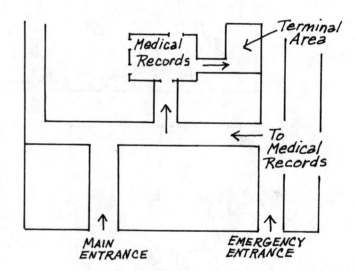

of them are quite sad. That seems strange to me, but maybe a hospital should have sad pictures on its walls.

When you open the door to Medical Records, you enter a small lobby. It looks like an office. There are several uncomfortable chairs, a desk, and a small table with a huge plant on it. On the walls, there are wooden boxes for incoming and outgoing medical charts. Four doors lead out of the lobby into the working areas.

I work in the file room, or "terminal area." My job description says that I am a "terminal operator." This is strange language for a hospital! To get to my area, take the right-hand door of the four. When you enter this door, you are in a small, cluttered hallway. It is quite different from the shiny, wide hallways outside. Along one side of this little hallway there are long counters. The counters are covered with papers and charts. Beyond the counters, there are large bookcases. On each shelf, there are white boxes, each one with a label. These boxes

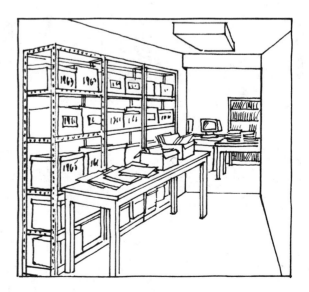

contain microfilm of patients' records for the past twenty-five years or so. Beyond the bookcases, there is another long counter. This is the sorting table, and it is usually piled high with charts that I need to file. Along the walls, there are metal carts like the ones in grocery stores. We use these to carry large numbers of charts around. Because we are so witty, we call them "chart carts."

My office is deep within the hospital. There are no windows. When I am inside, there is no way to know what is going on outside. There is no way to know whether it is day or night, rain or shine, war or peace. It is like working in a bomb shelter. I can't say that this office is my favorite place, except on payday, but it is very familiar to me.

Exercises on the Readings

EXERCISE A: COMPREHENSION

Please circle the letters below to show the correct answers. The information comes from Sebastian's and Cherry's essays in this unit. If you don't know an answer, go back to their essays.

1. When Sebastian was a child, he lived in
   a. the capital of Mexico.
   b. the capital of El Salvador.
   c. the capital of Honduras.

2. Sebastian's room had
   a. white walls and a wooden floor.
   b. white walls and a tile floor.
   c. blue walls and a wooden floor.

3. Through the window in his room, he was able to see
   a. the lights of Tegucigalpa.
   b. grass and trees.
   c. his neighbor's house.

4. In his room, there was some furniture:
   a. a bed, a desk with a chair, and a chest of drawers.
   b. two beds, a desk with two chairs, and a chest of drawers.
   c. two beds, a desk with a chair, and a dresser.

5. In Sebastian's room, he met
   a. the soccer star of Honduras!
   b. the Honduran Minister of Defense!
   c. the President of Honduras!

6. Cherry works
   a. in a wooden box.
   b. in a bomb shelter.
   c. in a hospital office.

7. To reach her office, you have to
   a. cross a parking lot.
   b. enter the emergency room.
   c. open four doors.

8. Cherry's office is

   a. small and cluttered.

   b. wide and shiny.

   c. dark and rainy.

9. In her office, there are

   a. counters, bookcases, a sorting table, and metal carts.

   b. beds, papers and charts, shopping carts, and bombs.

   c. wooden boxes, sad pictures, chairs, and a huge plant.

10. Cherry likes her office only when

   a. it rains.

   b. it's payday.

   c. it's clean.

EXERCISE B: PRESENT AND PAST TIME

Please complete the sentences below with verbs from the following list. Pay attention to the time and form of the verb. You may not need every form. The information comes from Sebastian's and Cherry's essays in this unit. Remember that Sebastian's information is about his childhood room, while Cherry's is about the office where she presently works.

PRESENT:	am/is/are	does/do	has/have	lives/live
PAST:	was/were	did	had	lived

1. Sebastian's room _____ on the second floor of the house where he lived in Tegucigalpa, Honduras.

2. Sebastian's family _____ in that house for ten years.

3. Sebastian's room _____ a large window.

4. Sebastian _____ his homework at the desk in his room.

5. Sebastian and his brother _____ in their room when their father introduced them to the President of Honduras!

6. Cherry _____ a part-time job in a hospital.

7. She _____ a "terminal operator." In plain English, this means that she files patients' records.

8. Cherry _____ her work in the file room of the Medical Records Office.

9. She works part-time, but she sometimes feels that she _____ at the hospital. She is thinking of putting a bed in one corner of her office and listing the hospital as her home address.

10. There _____ no windows in Cherry's office. She says that it is like a bomb shelter.

EXERCISE C: CAPITALIZATION

Please read the short essay below and add capital letters. The writer forgot all of them.

---

the library

maria and thomas are students at the university of new orleans. they are majoring in engineering. they are in the library now because they need to prepare for their afternoon classes. here is the scene.

in the front of the library, the librarian is standing behind the circulation desk. she is checking out books. several students are waiting to ask for information. others are waiting to check out books. nearby, quite a number of students are using the card catalog. they are looking for the call numbers of books that they need for their schoolwork.

across the room, students are waiting to use the copy machine. it is a popular machine. through the double glass doors, students are sitting at tables and desks. maria and thomas are studying at one of the tables. they often study together because they are good friends. besides, thomas likes maria to help him with his work. they seem to be studying hard. several students are resting in comfortable chairs. one is sleeping, and the other is reading a newspaper.

there are quite a few students in the back of the library. they are walking around the stacks and looking for books on the shelves. they are trying to find the books that they need for their classes. two of them are talking loudly to each other. other students are glaring at them. most students want the library to be a quiet place where they can concentrate on their work.

there is a lot going on in the library. it is a busy place. in some ways, it is the heart of the university. in other ways, it is like a busy train station.

Parallel Writing

Now that you have read Sebastian's and Cherry's essays, you are probably ready to write about one of your familiar places. Remember that your essay will be parallel to theirs, but not exactly the same. It may be shorter and simpler. Follow these instructions.

TALK WITH A PARTNER

1. Choose a partner (the same partner or a new one). Tell your partner about a familiar place. Describe it, using a lot of details. Try to make your partner see it in his or her mind. Make it as interesting as you can.

Your partner will take notes. After you finish talking, ask your partner to read the notes back to you. Did your partner understand everything? If not, explain it again, using different words.

2. Now it's your partner's turn. Listen and take notes. Then read your notes back to your partner. Make sure you have the correct information.

MAKE SOME DECISIONS

Before you write your essay, you need to make these decisions:

Who is your reader? (Choose a classmate.)

What does your reader want to know about your familiar place? (Think about what you and your partner talked about and write down some questions.)

WRITE A DRAFT

Write a draft of an essay about a place that is familiar to you. Answer the questions that you wrote, but don't write the questions. Write your sentences in paragraph form. As you write, you may get new ideas. Include them in your draft.

READ ALOUD TO YOUR PARTNER

1. Read your draft aloud to your partner. Your partner should listen carefully and think about these questions:

> Are all the details clear?
> Do they all belong?
> Are they presented in a good order?
> What else do I want to know?

Your partner may make comments while you read or after you finish reading. Remember that the purpose of these comments is to help you write better, not to say what is right and what is wrong. If your partner says that something is not clear, try writing it in a different way.

2. Ask your partner to read your draft to you. Listen with a stranger's ears. How does it sound? Can you picture the place clearly? Is there anything else that you want to say?

3. Now change roles with your partner. Listen to your partner's draft, talk about it, then read the draft aloud to your partner.

WRITE A SECOND DRAFT

Rework your essay. Remember that no piece of writing is ever really finished. Think about different ways to say the same idea. Look at Sebastian's and Cherry's essays. You may get some ideas that you can add to your draft.

EXCHANGE DRAFTS WITH YOUR READER

When you feel that your new draft is finished, give it to your reader. Your reader will give you his or her draft. You should read each other's drafts and write comments, such as:

> This is interesting.
> I don't understand this.
> This is a good detail.
> Can you tell me more about this?

Compare your reader's essay with yours. How is your familiar place different from your reader's?

REWRITE YOUR DRAFT

Look at your essay and your reader's comments carefully, then rewrite your essay one more time. Your teacher may want to read this final version and the drafts. Save both in your notebook.

Winding Down

Write a half-page in your learning log. Write to your teacher. Write about getting ideas. Do words come to you in English? In your native language? Both? Which activities do you find valuable? Working with a partner? Writing several drafts?

Write about these questions or other things that you want your teacher to know. Your teacher will read your writing, add some comments, and then return it to you to keep in your log.

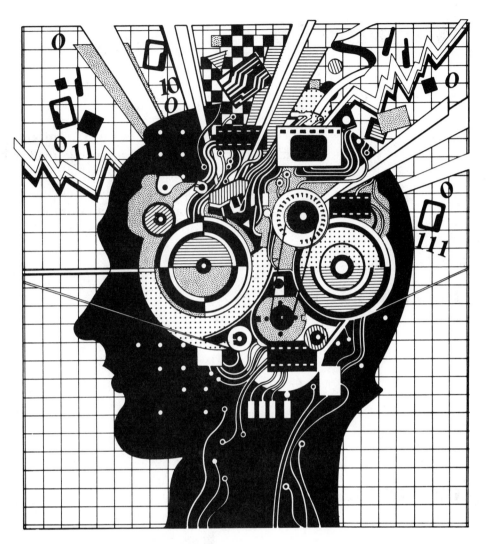

UNIT 9

TRAVELS

Rhetorical Focus: Narration

Organizational Focus: Chronological Order

Grammatical Focus: Simple Past Tense Review

Warming Up

YOUR JOURNAL

Write in your journal for five or ten minutes. Pretend that you are ready to go on a trip. Where are you going? Why are you going there? Is anybody going with you? What will you do and see?

Write words, phrases, and sentences. Write whatever comes to mind. Don't worry about correct grammar. If you can't think of anything, write "I don't know where I'm going." Keep writing it until something comes to mind.

PLAYING WITH WORDS

1. Write a list of five *silly things to take on a trip.*
   Example: a box of bricks
2. Write a list of five *crazy places to go on a vacation.*
   Example: the moon

Share your lists with your classmates.

GETTING READY TO READ

The essays in this unit are by Lien and Hassen. You may remember that Lien is from Taiwan and Hassen is from Tunisia. They are writing about trips that they once took. You are the reader. What do you want to know about their trips?

1. Write questions that you want them to answer about their trips.
   Example: Where did you go?
2. Write words that you expect Hassen and Lien to use in their essays.
   Example: went
             suitcase

Share your questions and words with your classmates.

Reading 9A

Please read about Lien's trip to Honduras:

DR. PEPPER, ANYONE?

Six years ago, I took a trip to Honduras. I went with my mother, sister, and brother. We went to visit my father, who was working there at the time. It was my first trip out of Taiwan.

I had my first taste of Western civilization on the airplane. The stewardesses were very kind, and I remember that they smiled a lot. They were the first foreigners that I had ever spoken to. I was fifteen then and spoke only Chinese. I knew two English words: "water" and "okay." I drank water all the way

from Taiwan to Honduras. That was no fun for a fifteen-year-old. When the stewardess said "Dr. Pepper," I thought she meant a person.

After the plane was in the air for a few hours, one of the stewardesses came around to each person and said a few words. I didn't understand the words, but somehow I knew that it was time for lunch. When she talked to me, I said "okay." I didn't know what I was going to have for lunch. I had chicken. For some reason, I ended up eating a lot of chicken. Other passengers ate steak.

This was just the beginning of many new experiences. Later, when I moved to the United States, I knew a little more English. By then, I was able to order all of the Dr. Pepper I wanted to drink!

Reading 9B

Please read about Hassen's adventure on the Mediterranean Sea:

A STORM AT SEA

One time, when I was a teenager, I decided to go with my father and his crew on a long fishing trip. My father was a fisherman, and he went on long trips all the time. My first trip with him turned out to be an adventure.

It was a cold winter morning when we set off. There was no wind and no need to put up the sails. My father started the engine, and we moved away from shore. I sat next to him as he held the rudder with both hands. Tiny clouds appeared in the sky, and a gentle breeze began to blow. My father asked the crew to put up the sails. I then went below to cook lunch for everyone.

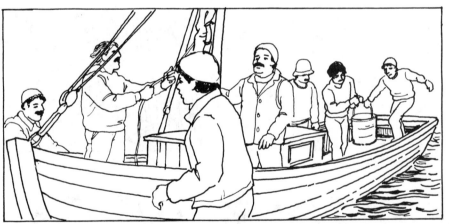

By the time lunch was ready, the sky was dark. The wind was stronger, and the waves were larger. We managed to eat lunch, and I then went below to clean up. As soon as I got below, the boat began to pitch from side to side. I heard my father yell to the crew to take down the sails. By the time I got back up on deck, a storm was raging. I held tight to the mast to stay on board. My father was fighting to keep control of the boat. Suddenly, I noticed that a barrel of gasoline was rolling across the deck. The gasoline was spilling in all directions. I knew that I had to stop it. With all my might, I pushed away from the mast and threw myself in the direction of the rolling bar-

rel. I fell on the barrel and hit my head against the deck. When I was able to move, I secured the barrel. Covered with gasoline, I crawled below. I fell on the bed, sick from the movement of the boat and the smell of gasoline. Somehow, I slept.

When I got up, it was night and the sea was calm. The storm was over. The sky was full of stars. At dawn, as the last star left the sky, the crew began to throw out the fishing nets. I suddenly understood something about my father. He was a brave man. He spent his days fighting the sea. A storm at sea was nothing unusual for him.

Exercises on the Readings

EXERCISE A: COMPREHENSION

Please circle the letters below to show the correct answers. The information comes from Lien's and Hassen's essays in this unit. If you don't know an answer, go back to their essays.

1. Six years ago, Lien went
   a. to Taiwan.
   b. to the United States.
   c. to Honduras.

2. She went there to visit
   a. Sebastian.
   b. her brother.
   c. her father.

3. On the airplane, Lien's problem was that
   a. she didn't speak English.
   b. she didn't like chicken.
   c. she didn't order any soft drinks.

4. She had chicken for lunch probably because
   a. she wanted chicken.
   b. the stewardesses served only chicken.
   c. she said "okay" when the stewardess said "Chicken?"

5. By the time Lien moved to the United States, she
   a. was sick of eating chicken.
   b. knew more English.
   c. liked Dr. Pepper.

6. Hassen's trip turned out to be
   a. an adventure.
   b. a bad dream.
   c. a fairy tale.

7. When Hassen left on his trip, it was
   a. a summer evening.
   b. a winter morning.
   c. a spring afternoon.

8. The boat began to pitch because
   a. there was a leak.
   b. one of the sails was torn.
   c. the waves were high.

9. Hassen fell on deck when he
   a. grabbed for the mast.
   b. tried to stop a rolling barrel.
   c. crawled below deck.

10. The storm was over
    a. by nightfall.
    b. by morning.
    c. by the next afternoon.

EXERCISE B: SIMPLE PAST TENSE

Both Lien and Hassen use a lot of past tense verbs in their essays. The simple forms of their verbs are given in the list below. Please write the simple past tense form for each one. Some are regular verbs and use -ed; some are not. If you have trouble, go back to their essays.

Example: take __**took**__

1. go _____
2. be _____
3. have _____
4. smile _____
5. speak _____
6. know _____
7. drink _____
8. say _____
9. think _____
10. mean _____
11. come _____
12. talk _____
13. end up _____
14. move _____

15. want _____
16. decide _____
17. turn out _____
18. set off _____
19. start _____
20. sit _____
21. hold _____
22. appear _____
23. begin _____
24. ask _____
25. manage _____
26. get _____
27. hear _____
28. notice _____

29. push _____   34. sleep _____

30. throw _____   35. leave _____

31. fall _____   36. understand _____

32. hit _____   37. spend _____

33. crawl _____

EXERCISE C: PAST TIME INFORMATION

Please answer the questions below about Lien and Hassen. The questions are about their trips. Write complete sentences.

Example: When did Lien take her trip?
She took it six years ago.

1. Where did Lien go?

_____

2. Why did she go there?

_____

3. How old was she?

_____

4. What language did she speak?

_____

5. Which English words did she know?

_____

6. Where did Hassen go?

_____

7. Who did he go with?

_____

8. What season of the year was it?

_____

9. What happened?

_____

10. What did Hassen learn about his father?

_____

Parallel Writing

Now that you have read about Lien's and Hassen's trips, you are probably ready to write about one of your own. Follow these instructions.

TEN QUESTIONS

For this unit, try a different activity: a game called Ten Questions.

1. Someone volunteers to be "it" (the teacher or class can choose someone). "It" should have a trip to tell about. (He or she can whisper it to the teacher first.)

2. The rest of the class forms teams of three or four people. Each team must think of ten questions about a trip, for example, "How long did you stay?"

3. The teams take turns asking "it" questions. The teams can ask a total of ten questions. The teacher writes the questions and answers on a piece of paper. Members of a team can also make notes. No question can be asked twice.

4. Members of each team have a minute or two to compare notes. Then the teacher asks the teams all the questions about the trip, and writes the answers on the board. "It" decides if an answer is correct.

5. The winner is the team that answers the most questions correctly.

MAKE SOME DECISIONS

Now, before you write about a trip, work alone to make these decisions:

Who is your reader? (Choose one.)

What does your reader want to know about your trip? (Think about the questions asked during the game; write them down.)

WRITE A DRAFT

Write a draft of an essay about a trip that you have taken. Answer the questions that you wrote, but don't write the questions. Write sentences in paragraph form. Use colorful details. As you write, you may get new ideas. Include them in your draft.

READ YOUR DRAFT TO YOURSELF

This time, read your draft to yourself. (You can try reading it aloud.) Think about these questions:

> Are all the details clear?
> Do they all belong?
> Are they presented in a good order?
> Is there anything else that I want to say?

WRITE A SECOND DRAFT

Rework your essay. Think about different ways to say something. Try to make it interesting. Look at Lien's and Hassen's essays. You may get some ideas that you can add to your draft.

EXCHANGE DRAFTS WITH YOUR READER

When you feel that your new draft is finished, give it to your reader. Your reader will give you his or her draft. You should read each other's drafts and write comments, such as:

> This is interesting.
> I don't understand this.
> Good detail.
> Can you write more about this?

Compare your reader's essay with yours. Are your trips very different?

REWRITE YOUR DRAFT

Look at your essay and your reader's comments. Then rewrite your essay one more time. Your teacher may want to read this final version and the drafts. Save both in your notebook.

Winding Down

Write a half-page in your learning log. Write to your teacher about this unit. Did you like the game? Why or why not? Did it help you with your essay? Do you prefer to work with a partner?

Write about these questions or other things that you want your teacher to know. Hand in the page to your teacher. He or she will read your writing, add some comments, and then return it to you to keep in your log.

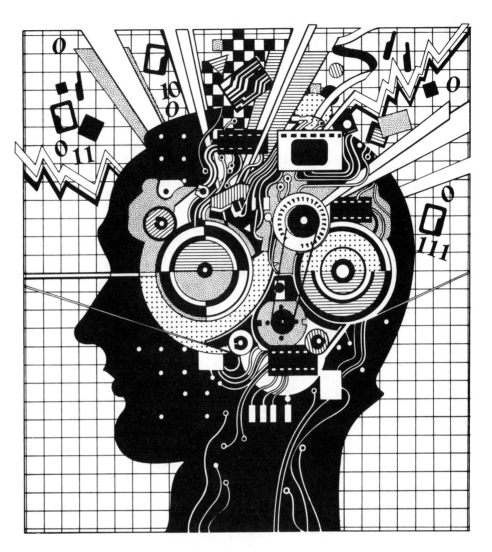

UNIT 10
UNUSUAL EVENTS

Rhetorical Focus: Narration

Organizational Focus: Chronological Order

Grammatical Focus: Simple Past Tense Review

Warming Up

YOUR JOURNAL

Write in your journal for five or ten minutes. Write about an unusual event: something strange, spooky, or frightening. Maybe it happened to you or to someone you know. Maybe someone just told you about it.

Write words, phrases, and sentences. Write whatever comes to mind. Don't worry about correct grammar. If you can't think of anything, write "I can't think of anything unusual to write about." Keep writing it until something comes to mind.

PLAYING WITH WORDS

1. Write five words that seem *strange* to you.

    Example: hippopotamus

2. List five *important events* in a person's life.

    Example: birth

Share your words with your classmates.

GETTING READY TO READ

The essays in this unit are by Hassen and Cherry. They are writing about unusual events in their lives. Both of their events are a little spooky. You are the reader. Are you curious? What do you want to know?

1. Write questions that you want them to answer about their unusual experiences.

    Example: When did this spooky event happen?

2. Write words that you expect them to use in their essays.

    Example: strange
            unusual

Share your questions and words with your classmates.

Reading 10A

Please read about something unusual that happened to Hassen's father:

THE WIZARD OF THE TOWN

In Tunisia, when something bad happens to a person, many people blame it on the "evil eye." The "evil eye" is a thing, a spirit, that hates and envies anything special. If a woman is very beautiful, she needs to watch out for the "evil eye." If a student is very intelligent, then watch out! Of course, I don't believe any of this, but many, many Tunisians do. Here is the story of my superstitious father, who lost his vision one day while he was out diving for sponges.

The day it happened, my father had collected more sponges than all the other fishermen. He was ready to come home when he suddenly saw only thick fog before his eyes. One of his crew

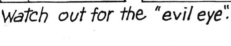
Watch out for the "evil eye".

had to lead him home. When he got home, I tried to talk him into seeing a doctor. My father was diabetic, and I was sure that his diabetes was causing his vision problem. *He* was sure that it was the evil eye.

My father wanted to see the town wizard, Mr. Belgacem, and I agreed to lead him to the wizard's house. Mr. Belgacem was about sixty years old, and he lived in an old house on the edge of town. When I asked him the secret of his power, he said, "Well, I've lived with my elf, Messaoud, since I was twenty or so. You cannot see him, but he is here. He is my gift from God."

My father sat down, and the wizard set a pan of burning coals in front of him. He put some leaves into the fire and began to mumble. As the smoke rose, I heard a whistling noise in the corner of the room. Then the wizard said, "There's Messaoud," and began to talk in a strange language. Since I don't

speak Elf, I didn't understand a word. Soon the noise stopped, and the wizard turned to my father. "It's too bad," he said, "but while you were diving for sponges, you stepped on a baby elf and killed it. To punish you, the mother elf caused your blindness. Messaoud thinks that it's the mother elf's fault that her baby died. She left her baby alone in a dangerous place. Messaoud has talked the mother into giving you back your sight, but she will not forgive you completely. In place of blindness, she will cause you to have bad dreams every night of your life." Mr. Belgacem said that he was sorry, but there was nothing more that he could do.

In a few days, my father's vision returned, but he began to have terrible dreams, just as the wizard predicted. To this day, he has bad dreams. Many times at night, I have heard him cry out in his sleep. My mother always wakes him up, but the dreams return as soon as he goes back to sleep. This story is hard to believe, but it is true.

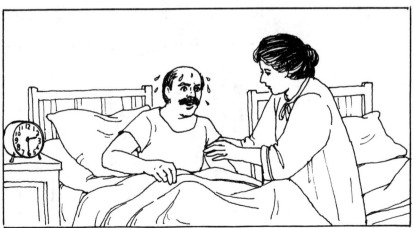

Reading 10B

Please read about something unusual that happened to Cherry:

BOO!

When I was eighteen, I worked for the editor of a small weekly newspaper, *The Red River Journal,* in Pineville, Louisiana. I was at work one Saturday on a special edition. The only other person there was my co-worker, Tanya. About eleven o'clock that morning, I had a strange experience.

I was walking down a long hallway when I heard someone call my name. I turned around to see a young man walking down the hallway a short distance behind me. I looked hard, because I was so sure that Tanya and I were the only ones in the office and the doors to the building were locked. In a second, the young man disappeared. Behind me, there was a dark-room, but it was at the end of the hall. It was impossible that the man was there, but I went to look anyway. I was more curi-

ous than scared, but I picked up a big can of roach spray as I entered the darkroom. As I expected, nobody was there. I decided not to tell Tanya; she was the nervous type.

Later that afternoon, I was hard at work at my desk when a hand fell on my shoulder. I screamed. It was only Tanya, who screamed, too. After we calmed down, she told me that she had just seen a woman at the door of her office. "I told her to wait just a minute," Tanya said, "and then, she disappeared." I decided then that it was time to tell Tanya about *my* ghost.

We decided to make a complete search of the building, but first we went for help. Next door, we found Mr. Wohlstaad, the owner of an engineering company, behind his desk. He was a strange, little man from Transylvania. Behind his back, we called him "The Count." We told him our story, and he agreed to accompany us on our search. Tanya and I picked up scissors as protection. The Count thought it was all a joke, and several times he jumped out in front of us and yelled "BOO!" After Tanya cut off his tie at the neck, he got the idea that we were serious.

We found nothing during our search and wasted an hour.

We finished our work as quickly as possible and left the building about 5:00 P.M. After a few glasses of Coke on our way home, we decided that we had imagined it all.

On Monday, we told the staff about our weekend experience. They laughed at us and teased us about ghosts for two weeks. Three weeks later, on a Wednesday afternoon, we were all working in the office, when Doc, our sports writer, yelled "Hey!" We all looked up, and there he was! As we watched, he took about five steps across the room and disappeared. I was almost happy to see him; at least, my co-workers knew that I wasn't crazy. My ghost showed up again twice that year, both times in front of at least three people. Tanya kept watching for her lady, but she never reappeared. I was glad. One ghost was enough.

Exercises on the Readings

EXERCISE A: COMPREHENSION

Please circle the letters below to show the correct answers. The information comes from Hassen's and Cherry's essays in this unit. If you don't know an answer, go back to their essays.

1. Many Tunisians believe that the "evil eye" is
   a. an elf that speaks a strange language.
   b. a spirit that envies anything special.
   c. a wizard.

2. When people believe that evil eyes, black cats, and broken mirrors will bring them bad luck, we say that they are
   a. superstitious.
   b. diabetic.
   c. envious.

3. Hassen's father
   a. went shopping.
   b. went for a walk.
   c. went blind.

4. Mr. Belgacem was
   a. a wizard.
   b. an elf.
   c. Hassen's neighbor.

5. Mr. Belgacem said that Hassen's father couldn't see because
   a. he was diabetic.
   b. he was a fisherman.
   c. he was responsible for the death of a baby elf.

6. Cherry had a strange experience while
   a. she was visiting Mr. Wohlstaad.
   b. she was working at the newspaper office.
   c. she was drinking wine with Tanya.

7. Cherry's ghost was
   a. a young woman.

b. a young man.

c. a child.

8. Mr. Wohlstaad was

a. the owner of the engineering company next door.

b. the ghost.

c. the editor of *The Red River Journal*.

9. Cherry and Tanya called Mr. Wohlstaad "The Count" because

a. he was tall and handsome.

b. he was from Transylvania and so was Count Dracula.

c. he wore neckties and black suits.

10. At first, Cherry's co-workers

a. believed her.

b. lied to her.

c. laughed at her.

EXERCISE B: SIMPLE PAST TENSE

Hassen and Cherry use many verbs in the simple past tense in their essays. Some of their verbs are listed below. Please write the simple form of each verb.

Example: lost _**lose**_

1. happened _____
2. saw _____
3. had to _____
4. got _____
5. tried _____
6. wanted _____
7. agreed _____
8. lived _____
9. asked _____
10. said _____
11. sat _____
12. began _____
13. rose _____

14. heard _____
15. stepped _____
16. killed _____
17. caused _____
18. died _____
19. left _____
20. returned _____
21. predicted _____
22. worked _____
23. thought _____
24. turned _____
25. looked _____
26. disappeared _____

27. went _____

28. picked _____

29. entered _____

30. expected _____

31. decided _____

32. fell _____

33. screamed _____

34. calmed _____

35. told _____

36. found _____

37. called _____

38. jumped _____

39. yelled _____

40. wasted _____

41. finished _____

42. left _____

EXERCISE C: PAST TIME EVENTS

Cherry says that she saw a ghost. You are from the office of Ghost Finders, Inc. and you are investigating. You need to understand the events on the day that Cherry saw the ghost. From Cherry's essay, determine exactly what happened (action by action) between 11:00 A.M. and 5:00 P.M. that day and write the actions in list form below. If you don't have enough room on this page, use another sheet of paper from your notebook.

1. Cherry walked down a long hallway at the newspaper office.

2. She heard someone call her name.

3. She turned around.

4. She saw a young man.

5. _____

6. _____

7. _____

8. _____

9. _____

10. _____

11. _____

12. _____

13. _____

14. _____

15. _____

Parallel Writing

Now that you have read about Hassen's and Cherry's unusual experiences, you may be ready to write about one of your own. Remember that your essay will be parallel to theirs, but not exactly the same. It may be shorter and simpler. Follow these instructions.

TWENTY QUESTIONS

For this unit, let's try a different game: Twenty Questions.

1. Someone volunteers to be "it." (The teacher or class can choose someone.) "It" should have an unusual event to tell about. (He or she can whisper it to the teacher first.)

2. Each person writes down at least ten "yes/no" questions to ask about the event. For example, "Did this event happen in your native country?" The answer can *only* be "yes" or "no."

3. Individual students take turns asking "it" questions. The class can ask no more than twenty questions. After twenty questions (or before), students can try to guess what happened and tell the rest of the class. "It" decides if the story is correct. If no one can guess, then "it" tells the story.

MAKE SOME DECISIONS

Now, before you write about an unusual experience, work alone to make these decisions:

Who is your reader? (Choose one.)

What does your reader want to know about your unusual experience? (Think about the questions asked during the game; write them down.)

WRITE A DRAFT

Write a draft of an essay about an unusual event. Answer the questions that you wrote, but don't write the questions. Write your sentences in paragraph form. Use colorful details. As you write, you may get new ideas. Include them in your draft.

READ YOUR DRAFT

Read your draft to yourself or work with a partner. Either way, think about these questions:

> Are all the details clear?
> Is anything not clear?
> Is there anything else that I want to say?

WRITE A SECOND DRAFT

Rework your essay. Think about different ways to say the same idea. Try to make it interesting. Look at Hassen's and Cherry's essays. They may give you some ideas that you can add to your draft.

EXCHANGE DRAFTS WITH YOUR READER

When you feel that your new draft is finished, give it to your reader. Your reader will give you his or her draft. You should read each other's drafts and write comments.

Compare your reader's essay with yours. Are your experiences similar or different?

REWRITE YOUR DRAFT

Look at your essay and your reader's comments carefully. Then rewrite your essay one more time. Your teacher may want to read this final version and the drafts. Save both in your notebook.

Winding Down

Write a half-page or more in your learning log. Write to your teacher about this course. Did you learn a lot? What was especially valuable? Was there anything that you didn't like? Do you have any ideas about how to make the course better?

Write about these questions or other things that you want your teacher to know. Hand in the page to your teacher. He or she will read your writing, make some comments, and then return it to you to keep in your log.